IT HAPPENED IN
DENVER

Stephen Grace

TWODOT®

GUILFORD, CONNECTICUT
HELENA, MONTANA
AN IMPRINT OF THE GLOBE PEQUOT PRESS

A · TWODOT® · BOOK

Copyright © 2007 Morris Book Publishing, LLC

Text design by Nancy Freeborn
Front cover photo: Snow cuts on Rollins Pass, Moffat Road, 1904. Denver Public Library, Western History Collection, Louis Charl McClure, MCC-450
Back cover photo: Denver, 1913. Denver Public Library, Western History Collection, x-28974

Library of Congress Cataloging-in-Publication Data
Grace, Stephen.
  It happened in Denver/Stephen Grace.—1st ed.
      p. cm.—(It happened in series)
  Includes bibliographical references.
  ISBN-13: 978-0-7627-4129-8
  ISBN-10: 0-7627-4129-5
  1. Denver (Colo.)—History—Anecdotes. I. Title.
  F784.D457G73 2007
  978.8'83—dc22

                                                           2006026998

Manufactured in the United States of America
First Edition/First Printing

CONTENTS

CONTENTS

PREFACE

I am a psychologist by training, a novelist by profession, and I make no claims to be a professional historian. I am simply a Colorado resident fascinated with the lore of my state's capital city. My book has been thoroughly researched, but *It Happened in Denver* is in no way meant to be scholarly or comprehensive. It is intended to tell a handful of fascinating stories.

No one could argue that Denver has been without its flaws. Like the nation of which it is a part, Denver has been plagued by episodes of hatred and injustice. In my book I have tried to find a balance between stories that tell some of the more disturbing parts of the city's history, such as the Hop Street Riot, in which racially motivated anger led to violence, and stories that demonstrate some of Denver's finest moments, such as the glorious rebirth of its Lower Downtown district. Denver, much like its citizens, has never been perfect but has always been interesting.

The events I have chosen to write about do not tell the whole story of Denver's past, but they do illustrate some of the themes that run throughout the city's history: a legacy of lawlessness; a pioneer spirit that refuses to give up when faced with seemingly insurmountable odds; a tradition of taking bold gambles on the city's future; and a cycle of highs and lows as dramatic as the topography of the Rockies, as thrilling as a ride at downtown Denver's Elitch Gardens.

Enjoy the ride.

ACKNOWLEDGMENTS

I would like to thank Denver's professional historians for performing the sometimes thankless task of delving into the past and telling the truth. I am grateful to the dedicated and hardworking staffs of the Denver Public Library, the Colorado Historical Society, Byers-Evans House Museum, The Molly Brown House, and Historic Denver, Inc.

Cheers to David French and Aron Rosenthal of the Orbis Institute for their friendship and for working tirelessly to prepare Denver's youth for an increasingly global world. The Orbis Institute is keeping alive Denver's proud traditions of generous philanthropy and bold social entrepreneurship; the efforts of Mr. French and Mr. Rosenthal are reminiscent of the worthy struggles of a true pioneer from Denver's history, Emily Griffith.

Many thanks to my editors, Patrick Straub and Allen Jones, for their encouragement and support.

Most of all I'd like to thank my wife, Amy, for her patience, her honesty, and her good sense—and for putting up with my incessant ramblings about tales from Denver's past.

THE PIKES PEAK GOLD RUSH

- 1859 -

A DECADE AFTER THE CALIFORNIA GOLD RUSH, William Russell crouched down next to an icy stream and peered into his pan. A smile stretched across his weather-beaten face as he realized he'd finally found what he'd been searching for. GOLD! Though he had panned only a few handfuls of yellow flakes, the Great Pikes Peak Gold Rush was on.

The precious metal may previously have been discovered near the site of present-day Denver by Spanish explorers looking for El Dorado, a legendary city of fabulous wealth. But if conquistadors did in fact return from the Rockies with a few small samples of gold, it's no wonder their discoveries didn't lead to further exploration: The Spanish were searching for a city made of gleaming metal, not gold dust and nuggets scattered amid mountain streams.

United States explorer Zebulon Pike was told by a trapper that there was gold in the mountains where the South Platte River originated; Pike included this information in a report of his exploration of the region, but it didn't lead to the excitement of a gold rush. Nor did reports of gold by other early explorers lead to further investigation—claims of gold discoveries were common but rarely proved true, and the place where Denver was to grow was in the heart of the "Great American Desert," an area considered harsh and inhospitable, a great blank space on maps.

But this indifference changed when William Green Russell, a Georgian who'd worked in the California goldfields in the heyday of the California Gold Rush, heard of a group of Cherokee who claimed they had found gold when they'd paused in their travels to rest by the South Platte River. They spread the word about their find when they returned to Oklahoma, but no one acted on the information until Russell learned of it almost a decade later. Russell was married to a Cherokee woman. Members of her tribe told him tales of gold that stoked his fever for quick wealth.

Russell talked his brothers and six other companions into joining him, and they set off in search of the rumored gold. Along the way they met up with members of the Cherokee tribe on the banks of the Arkansas River in present-day Oklahoma. As they continued west along the Santa Fe Trail, they were joined by other groups, and the ranks of William Russell's band of gold seekers soon grew to more than one hundred.

When they reached the confluence of Cherry Creek and the South Platte near present-day Denver, they immediately began prospecting in the chilly waters of Cherry Creek and Ralston Creek, but they found no gold. After twenty days without success, most of the men grew disgruntled and decided to return home, leaving Russell, his two brothers, and ten other men behind. Undaunted, Russell's skeleton crew continued to prospect, and finally, at the mouth of Little Dry Creek where it spilled into the South Platte, they discovered "good diggings."

A wandering trader visited the Russell party shortly after their discovery. He left with a sack of pay dirt, and when he reached Kansas City, he panned it before a crowd, revealing glittering flakes of the coveted metal. Rumors began. Traders and mountain men told exaggerated tales of Russell's find, and word spread like wildfire throughout the Mississippi River Valley and farther east. Citizens jammed meetings in town halls to learn of the discovery. Newspapers filled the void of real information with enthusiastic headlines: "Gold Excitement on the Increase," "Kansas Gold Fever," "Gold! Gold!! Gold!!! Gold!!!! Hard to Get and Heavy to Hold. Come to Kansas!!" (Present-day Denver is located in what was then the Kansas Territory.)

When men with nothing to lose learned of the discovery, they came to Denver on horseback and they came in wagons—some even came on foot, pushing all their worldly belongings in wheelbarrows. The owner of a "wind wagon" with a sail promised passengers his contraption would get them to the goldfields ahead of the swarms of fortune seekers, but the wind-powered wagon crashed in a gully soon after beginning its westward journey.

Pikes Peak, a rugged fourteen-thousand-foot mountain south of Denver, became an emblematic landmark for argonauts in search of rich deposits. By the spring of 1859 masses of prospective miners with "PIKES PEAK OR BUST!" written on their wagons were heading west to set up camp in the Denver area. Observers in towns along the Mississippi noted that roads leading west from the river were "white with the wagons of Pikes Peak emigrants." As Americans were mesmerized by get-rich-quick dreams and tales of the precious metal, "Pikes Peak" became a household term throughout the United States. *The St. Louis News* reported in March of 1859: "[Pikes Peak] is the magnet to the mountains, toward which everybody and everything is tending. It seems that every man, woman and child, who is going anywhere at all, is moving Pike's Peakward." Some enterprising souls along the westward trails made fortunes for themselves by writing and selling guidebooks describing how to make a fortune in gold.

Like the forty-niners who had flocked to California's goldfields a decade earlier, hordes of fifty-niners headed to Denver to get rich. Tents and tarps sprang up virtually overnight among the cottonwood groves on the banks of the South Platte River. Soon crude cabins were raised, and a makeshift town amid the teepees of the Arapaho began to sprawl along the rolling plains. For the next two years, gold fever gripped the eastern states and more than one hundred thousand fifty-niners pioneered across the parched and sprawling wilds of the Great American Desert to begin new lives. As with the card players who filled Denver's burgeoning saloons and gambling halls, these immigrants were risking everything on a bet: They were gambling that they'd find abundant gold and in a few short months accumulate the wealth that would have taken them a lifetime of work in the East to earn.

As the westward migration increased, newspaper editors in the East began to wonder why no gold had been shipped back by prospectors. Soon the first reports of "go-backers" appeared in the papers. Faced with grim living conditions and hard work, would-be miners were fleeing the territory. Fortune hunters who had panned along the South Platte but had found nothing except gravel and dirt started intercepting the thousands of wagons that had traveled halfway to Denver. Bitter about being duped, the disgruntled prospectors convinced many of the new gold seekers to turn around. During what the *Rocky Mountain News* called "the insane rush back," some desperate souls in Denver built boats and tried to float down the South Platte to return home. Many of the boats wrecked amid the Platte's turbulent waters, drowning their passengers.

But just as newspapers back East began running stories about the "Great Bamboozle" and decrying the stories of Rocky Mountain gold as "a hoax" and "humbug," big strikes were made by persistent prospectors who ventured into the hills. Significant quantities of the precious metal were discovered at Idaho Springs and Central City in the Rockies west of Denver, what the Arapaho called "the shining mountains." Denver's population swelled along the plains as it grew into a substantial town to serve the nearby gold mines. Enterprising Denverites built businesses based on "mining the miners," encouraging prospectors to spend their new wealth on prostitution, drink, and gambling. The massive migration of white settlers to Denver uprooted the Native Americans who inhabited the land around the South Platte, and it caused the first of many booms in the area, giving birth to the city's reputation as a rowdy Wild West town filled with people seeking quick and easy riches.

THE RISE OF JUDGE LYNCH

- 1859 -

Tom Pollock, known around Denver as "Noisy Tom," thumbed back the wide brim of his hat and watched a group of gangsters who were roaming the town's dirt streets. The men wandered into a restaurant. Tom walked up to a window of the restaurant and watched as the armed thugs inside gorged themselves, refused to pay, and then dared the owner to stop them. Tom shook his head and put his hand on a holstered pistol. He was fed up with the lack of order in this town. There was no sheriff, no town marshal. It was up to men like him to stop gangsters from ruining Denver.

One resident of early Denver stated that the town was overrun with characters "soured in temper, always armed, bristling at a word, ready with the rifle, revolver or bowie knife." Stores were robbed in broad daylight, and heavily armed hordes of hooligans preyed at will on the innocent and the weak.

One particularly bizarre episode of thuggery occurred around Christmastime of 1859 when turkey thieves invaded the town, stealing a wagonload of fowls. Denver's respectable citizens had finally had enough. A citizens' meeting was called. Speeches were made demanding the gang of turkey thieves, known as the "Bummers," be dealt with. All "respectable" men in town armed themselves with revolvers and rifles. The Bummers, wielding guns and bowie knives, paraded through town, defying the people of Denver to challenge them. The blacksmith named "Noisy Tom" Pollock did just that. Known for his commanding voice, Noisy Tom cracked one of the gangsters across the head with the barrel of his rifle, killing him. Following Pollock's example, a posse of vigilantes threatened the rest of the turkey-stealing hoodlums with hanging if they didn't leave town. The thieves fled, ending Denver's "Turkey War" and giving rise to vigilantism.

Shortly after the Turkey War ended, a barkeeper named James Gordon killed an unarmed man. Gordon fled Denver to Leavenworth, Kansas, but friends of the murdered man tracked Gordon down and beat him almost to death. They dragged him in chains back to Denver, where Gordon faced the People's Court, which had no legitimate legal authority to pass sentence or to mete out punishment. Nevertheless, the court decided Gordon should be hanged, and four days later he swung from a tree. By the standards of frontier justice, this was not necessarily swift punishment. John Stoefel, for instance, had been killed within forty-eight hours of his conviction. After shooting his brother-in-law over disputed gold dust, Stoefel had been dragged from jail by a mob and hanged from a cottonwood tree.

The executions of Gordon and Stoefel marked the rise of what became known as "Judge Lynch": violent justice dispensed without the rule of law by angry mobs and vengeful gangs. Soon the bodies of accused criminals, their presumed offences ranging from horse stealing to murder to sex crimes, dangled from cottonwoods throughout Denver.

Denver appointed a town marshal, Noisy Tom Pollock of Turkey War fame. Pollock received fifty cents for every criminal he caught, and he locked them up in a hotel he'd built. Legend has it he used "lead-poisoning" and "rope-burn" to punish the more dangerous of the lawbreakers during his brief tenure as town marshal. He pleaded for help housing Denver's many scoundrels, but Denver refused to build a jail and Pollock resigned after only five months as marshal.

A spate of homicides followed. A newspaper describing a new hotel, the first in Denver to feature locks on the doors, reported, "Guests may lie down to peaceful slumbers, undisturbed by the apprehensions of getting their heads blown off." Desperate for some sort of order to take hold in the town, Denver appointed a police force of four men, but the officers failed to stop the tide of murders sweeping town.

The crisis of lawlessness came to a head when William Byers, the editor of the *Rocky Mountain News,* was kidnapped from his newspaper's headquarters in retaliation for an article he'd printed lashing out against criminals. The kidnappers took Byers to the nearby Criterion saloon where he managed to escape after a bartender gave him a pistol and showed him a back door. Byers' attackers again came after him but he barricaded himself in his newspaper office with several shotgun-wielding friends. A kidnapper named George Steele galloped by the office on a horse and fired through a window. Steele's bullet whizzed past Byers. A shotgun blast from inside the building caught Steele in his hip and made him slump in his saddle. When Tom Pollock, who happened to be in his nearby blacksmith shop, heard the commotion, he ran outside and filled Steele with buckshot. As Steele toppled from his horse, the rest of the kidnappers fled.

After the attack on Byers, Denver's citizens took matters into their own hands, and "Judge Lynch" again presided over the land.

Warnings were issued to troublemakers by giving them scraps of paper bearing a sketch of a tree with a man dangling from one of its branches above a scribbled command such as "Clear out by 6 A.M., or—." A vigilante committee of Denver's citizens captured people they thought had committed crimes. Following a short trial they were hung in public, often in daylight, while crowds of men, women, and children looked on.

The fear of hanging proved a potent crime deterrent. After several episodes of frontier-style justice, thugs were no longer terrorizing the town, and Denver's citizens rested a bit easier knowing that order—even though it was not accompanied by law—had finally been established.

Vigilantism in Denver began to decline when the United States Government formed the Colorado Territory in 1861, bringing the entire area, including Denver, into the federal fold. The People's Court of Denver disbanded. Legitimate courts were set up and judges were selected. Justice at the end of a noose and without the benefit of due process fell out of favor. Public hangings were soon outlawed and the rule of law supplanted mob rule in the streets of Denver. The town's legacy of lynching didn't die easily, however. "Judge Lynch" continued his ghastly work, often at night, in mining camps and rural areas around Denver where victims of mob execution were counted well into the twentieth century.

THE FOUNDING OF A FRONTIER MINT

- 1860 -

TWO BROTHERS, AUSTIN AND MILTON CLARK, WATCHED from their barstools in a Denver saloon as a miner reached into his buckskin poke. He took out a pinch of gold dust, put it in the palm of a bartender's hand, and asked for a shot of Taos Lightning. Both brothers noticed a few glittering flakes fall from the bartender's hand as he reached for a whiskey bottle. They looked at each other and nodded. They knew that the town needed a mint and they knew they could make a mint for themselves by building it.

Miners who struck it rich in the goldfields had a problem. When they came down from the mountains into Denver, they had to convert the precious metal they'd found into currency they could use to purchase food and supplies. There was little coinage and paper money in the frontier town. At first gold dust was only used in the occasional barter, but soon it became the main medium of exchange.

A miner would place a pinch or two atop a counter in a general store and, in return, he was given the flour he needed or the whiskey he craved. A pinch between thumb and forefinger (regardless of the size of the thumb and forefinger doing the pinching) represented "two bits" (twenty-five cents). Larger denominations were dumped out and measured on scales. Miners usually lost out on the deal by overpaying for goods. A lot of gold was fumbled by clumsy fingers, and much of the fine dust stuck to pouches or shopkeepers' scales, or sifted between boards. Thrifty pioneers swept their floors with turkey-feather brooms to recover piles of gold dust. Saloon floors and the floors beneath theater ticket windows were particularly rich sources for spilled gold.

Crooks mixed dust of dubious origin such as heavy brass filings with the pricey yellow powder; con men covered chunks of brass with a thin layer of gold and bought their grub and whiskey with these phony nuggets. Dishonest merchants altered their scales so they could cheat miners. Bickering over the size and value of a pinch led to arguments that were often settled with fists or guns. Robberies occurred in broad daylight outside the town's most popular watering hole, Uncle Dick Wootton's saloon.

In addition to the many problems associated with measuring gold dust and using it for commerce, the raw gold had to be shipped to far-away federal mints so that it could be converted into coins. The cost to transport the gold was high, and the stagecoaches carrying the valuable cargo had to pass through long stretches of prairie filled with bandits.

Three resourceful businessmen set out to solve the gold dust problem. After doing extensive research and determining that private mints were not illegal in the United States, two enterprising brothers, Austin and Milton Clark, joined with Emanuel Gruber. They built one of the early city's most substantial structures, a two-story brick bank building on the northwest corner of McGaa and G Streets (now Sixteenth and Market). After purchasing dies, coin presses, and other minting machinery from suppliers in the East, Clark, Gruber & Company transported this cargo by railroad and ox team to Denver and set up shop in the basement of their bank. They capitalized on the town's desperate need for coinage by buying raw gold from miners and then stamping that gold into coins. To ensure that everyone was satisfied with the value of their product, they added a little more gold than federal coins contained.

In July 1860, the new mint began stamping $10 coins. To the delight of onlookers, glittering coins with "PIKES PEAK GOLD" marked above an image of the famous mountain rode down a conveyor belt and clinked into a bucket. The very first coin minted was given as a gift to the editor of the *Rocky Mountain News,* which publicized the event.

When the $10 coins went over well in Denver, and both miners and merchants seemed satisfied with the new currency, Clark, Gruber & Company went on to make $2.50, $5, and $20 pieces. By October 1860 their private mint had produced a total of $120,000 in gold coins. They continued to mint sizable quantities of gold coins and also produce paper notes that could be exchanged for their gold coins, in great demand all over Denver. Clark, Gruber & Company quickly developed a reputation for honesty, and their business was considered beyond reproach.

Though the private mint provided a valuable service to Denver and proved to be very profitable for its owners, it was short-lived. When politicians in the Colorado Territory decided to advocate for opening a United States Government branch mint in Denver, the Clark brothers and Gruber supported this, fearing that the private minting of coins came very close to being illegal. Though what they were doing was currently not forbidden by United States law, the savvy trio of entrepreneurs knew that the days of private mints were numbered.

Austin Clark accompanied the territorial delegate for Colorado to Washington, D.C. A poke filled with gold dust was given to Congress, and a gold snuffbox was gifted to the Speaker of the House. Clark and Gruber coins were sent to Philadelphia for testing and analysis. They received good reviews, and the United States treasury secretary asked Congress to authorize a branch mint in Denver. He recommended that the building, equipment, and machinery of the Clark, Gruber & Co. Mint be purchased immediately by the government to get the new branch up and running as soon as possible. A bill to create a United States mint in Denver was passed by both houses of Congress. President Lincoln added his signature to make it official, and the United States Denver Mint was born.

When the new United States Mint and Assay Office at Denver opened for business, nuggets and dust brought to the mint by miners were melted, assayed, and stamped into cast gold bars. The bars were then returned to the miners marked with the weight and fineness of the gold. Unlike Clark, Gruber & Company, however, the federal mint performed no coinage of gold as Congress had intended. This was due to fears of banditry on the frontier when loads of valuable coins were transported across the plains. The reason given by the director of the mint for the lack of coinage was, "the hostility of the Indian tribes along the routes, doubtless instigated by rebel emissaries (there being a Civil War) and bad white men."

Eventually the mint was moved to a new building on West Colfax Avenue and Cherokee Street. The original building became the home of a vegetable business, and, after an industrious Denverite recovered gold dust from the dirt floor, the basement where gold coins had once been stamped was turned into a storehouse for potatoes and onions.

Not until after the mint machinery had been sent to the St. Louis World's Fair for display did coinage operations finally begin in the new building. Presses struck coins with a "D" mint mark to be circulated among the American public. During the first year of production,

167 million coins were produced, including gold "eagles" that had the likeness of an eagle on one side. The mint made $20 gold (double eagle) coins, $10 gold (eagle) coins, $5 gold (half-eagle) coins, as well as silver coins.

Several rare dates of Denver Mint coins are popular with collectors, and original Clark, Gruber & Company gold coins are highly prized—only about one thousand of them are known to exist. Today, the Denver branch of the United States Mint is one of the world's major producers of official legal-tender coins, and it is the country's second-largest gold-bullion depository.

GILPIN'S GAMBLE TO
SAVE THE UNION

- 1862 -

In the early winter of 1862 as a blizzard swirled through the sky, a volunteer army departed Denver. Trudging through deepening snow, the men climbed into the mountains. Though they were exhausted and cold, they couldn't stop marching. The fate of the Union depended on them crossing Raton Pass.

Just six weeks after Colorado became a territory, the Civil War began. Confederate sympathizers flew a rebel flag over a store in Denver; Unionists tore it down. Most Denverites had emigrated to the West from northern states, so the majority of the town's citizens were loyal to the Union. Denver's first mayor, however, was a Confederate. When the Civil War began, he fled Denver and returned to the South.

William Gilpin, a strong defender of the Union, was appointed Colorado's first territorial governor by President Abraham Lincoln. Afraid that Confederate sympathizers within Colorado would attack the territory and that Confederate Texans would take over the Southwest and then head north toward Rocky Mountain goldfields—and even afraid that his own life might be in danger from Confederates lurking in Colorado—Gilpin decided to act immediately and worry about the consequences later. He raised Union volunteers, most of them miners from the mountains around Denver, and issued $375,000 in federal promissory notes to pay for the formation of the First Regiment of Colorado Volunteer Infantry. Though Gilpin lacked the authority to issue these promissory notes, he believed the United States Government would gladly honor them because the notes were being used to finance the defense of the Union.

Initially, most Colorado citizens went along with the governor's campaign for military preparedness. The few who objected were quieted when Gilpin suggested that the alternative to issuing the promissory notes was for the government to simply confiscate needed supplies from citizens. Still, rumors about the notes not having any real value spread throughout Denver, and Gilpin's unpopularity continued to grow, finally reaching a crisis point when the federal government announced that it would not honor the promissory notes. Gilpin protested that President Lincoln had given him verbal permission to issue the notes. But the United States Government did not relent, and Denver's shopkeepers, store owners, and businesspeople who had been paid for their goods with the promissory notes, now worth no more than the paper Gilpin's staff had printed them on, were furious. As the Denver economy spiraled downward toward depression, irate citizens circulated petitions in Denver and throughout the rest of Colorado calling for Gilpin's immediate removal from the governorship. Gilpin went to Washington to plead his case in person.

Regardless of the legitimacy and true value of the promissory notes, they made it possible to equip the First Regiment of Colorado Volunteer Infantry. For several months the regiment had been training at Fort Weld on the outskirts of Denver. When Gilpin went to Washington to explain himself to the federal government, the regiment, now ten companies strong, was well equipped and well trained. They were ready for action.

That action came shortly. In the winter of 1862 while Gilpin was still in Washington, one of his fears was realized—the Confederate Army began moving across the Southwest toward Denver. Confederate General Henry Hopkins Sibley raised a brigade of mounted Texas riflemen and launched the Confederate's New Mexico Campaign by taking the city of Santa Fe. He was also preparing to attack Fort Union in northern New Mexico Territory. The only obstacle between General Sibley's Confederate Brigade and Denver's goldfields was Fort Union, an army depot on the Santa Fe Trail. If the rebels seized the supplies and weapons kept at Fort Union, they could continue their march north to Denver and be able to prevent troops in the Colorado Territory from harassing them as they set up an overland route through New Mexico and Arizona that would link them with Confederate sympathizers in California. In short, if Confederate soldiers captured Denver and controlled its goldfields, they would dominate the entire West, and they would use Denver's mineral wealth to finance the defeat of the Union. Denver was the lynchpin in the rebels' scheme to take over the West—and ultimately the entire country.

But Denver's scrappy volunteer army was not about to let this happen without a fight. The First Regiment left Denver, and in a mere thirteen days it marched 400 miles and through deep snow on Raton Pass to Fort Union. While resupplying and resting there, the First Regiment, under the command of Colonel John P. Slough, a Denver attorney turned soldier, was joined by some United States Army troops and New Mexico volunteers. The bolstered First Regiment left Fort Union and followed the Santa Fe Trail to meet the

Confederate Army. They set up camp east of Glorieta Pass, a strategic gap in the Sangre de Cristo Mountains. Early Spanish explorers had named the mountains for the "Blood of Christ," but the blood that was spilled during the Battle of Glorieta Pass was from Union troops and Confederate soldiers.

After three days of fierce fighting around Glorieta Pass, the Confederates took possession of the battlefield. The Confederate leader, believing he had won, was forced to reconsider when he received news that a Union force, led by Major John M. Chivington of the Colorado First Regiment, had left the battlefield to find the Confederate supply train. Chivington's men had driven off the Confederate guards, killed horses and mules, destroyed artillery, taken prisoners, and burned wagons containing ammunition, food, and clothing. Lacking supplies, the rebels could no longer continue their march on Fort Union, and ultimately Denver. Major Chivington was hailed as the hero of the battle as the Confederate army retreated to Santa Fe and ended its New Mexico Campaign.

The Battle of Glorieta Pass, with the Colorado's First Regiment's clever attack on the Confederate supply train, had decided once and for all that Denver's goldfields would remain with the Union, and it put an end to the Confederacy's dreams of taking over the West. As one Texan put it, "If it had not been for those devils from Pikes Peak, this country would have been ours." Historians have dubbed the pivotal battle "The Gettysburg of the West."

Even though the Union victory at Glorieta Pass seemed to vindicate Gilpin's decision to act quickly and decisively to finance a fighting force, citizens of Denver didn't see it that way, and Gilpin's federal promissory notes dealt his political career a blow from which it never recovered. The federal treasury of the United States Government eventually decided to reimburse people who had been paid with the notes, but this decision came too late to revive the political fortunes of Gilpin. Perhaps because of his paranoia that all his political opponents were rebel sympathizers bent on assassinating him, perhaps because he'd angered the powerful editor of Denver's *Rocky Mountain News* by appointing the territorial printing contract to a rival newspaper, or perhaps simply because the Denver economy had been dealt such a severe blow by promissory notes tying up most of its circulating currency, the majority of Denver's citizens clamored for Gilpin's removal. In April 1862, President Lincoln stripped him of his governorship. William Gilpin had saved the Union, but he couldn't save his career.

THE GREAT FIRE

- 1863 -

On April 19 at two o'clock in the morning, while most of Denver slept, ferocious winds hissed and roared, drowning all other sounds. In the bars along Blake Street, the noise of late-night revelers was buried beneath the howling wind. Even the screams of "FIRE!" when a man kicked over a stove at the Cherokee House saloon were only heard by a few.

Early Denver was an insurance agent's nightmare. Most of the city's downtown consisted of structures that had been hastily built of native pine—a wood filled with highly flammable pitch. Denver's downtown buildings were little more than shacks. A few of them "towered" to two stories, but most of them were a single story and had a false front to make them look taller than they actually were. They were crammed tightly together. As one citizen noted, buildings in the business district "stood cheek by jowl without room for a yellow cat to squeeze between them." Most of the homes in the area were log cabins. A few houses built by Denver's wealthy elite were made of wooden frames. Roofs on all of the houses were made of wooden shingles. Downtown Denver was a giant tinderbox. All that was needed to start a disastrous fire was a spark and wind.

Denver had understood the extreme fire danger of the city early on in its development. Throughout the West devastating fires were a regular occurrence. William Byers, the editor of the *Rocky Mountain News,* was one of the first of Denver's citizens to campaign for fire equipment and a trained and professional force to operate it. Aside from the flammability of Denver's downtown there was another problem—Denver was filled with "firebugs," people who deliberately started blazes to make a moral or political statement. And there was no shortage of careless drunken revelers in Denver's many bars, all of them filled with candles and oil lamps. Byers used the newspaper to educate people about the fire dangers of Denver and the need to create a professional fire department.

People listened. The city council prohibited the construction of any new buildings made of wood; they passed ordinances that provided for the inspection of stoves and fireplaces; they prohibited the storage of straw and hay within forty feet of any structure. The council purchased a hook-and-ladder and organized two bucket brigades. They passed an ordinance that said citizens present at a fire had to help—failure to pitch in could lead to fines of up to five dollars and jail time. It was a start. But a trained force of fully equipped professional firefighters was still a long way off, and downtown Denver was still being filled with wooden buildings, despite a city ordinance prohibiting their construction.

An alderman and business owner put a roof from an old building on a new wood building, trying to pass it off as old and exempt from the ordinance. He was fined fifty dollars. Outraged, he lobbied the city council to repeal the ordinance. The council, which consisted of many business associates of the alderman, did exactly that. After they repealed the ordinance, slews of flammable shacks were quickly built downtown.

After a series of fires broke out in brothels along the city's Riverfront District, it was rumored that the blazes had been started by firebugs protesting the immorality of houses of prostitution in their city. The *Weekly Commonwealth and Republican* warned in an editorial that if a house or building were set afire on a windy night "every house in Denver will be level with the ground in three hours." The newspaper issued another warning after a fire broke out one midnight in February of 1863. Only the quick work of several hundred men—and a lack of high winds to fan the flames—stopped it from turning into a disastrous blaze and burning nearby buildings. The newspaper said the men had been lucky, and it was only a matter of time before a catastrophic fire ravaged the city. They were right.

When the April 19 fire at the Cherokee House Saloon began, drinkers shouted as flames were spread by wind. Their panicked cries woke up some sleepers in buildings around the blaze but most residents of Denver weren't aware of the fire until the next morning, when they woke to find the heart of the city's business district in piles of smoking ash.

The strong winds that were blowing on the night of April 19 were a mixed blessing. Because of their direction they prevented the fire from spreading to the west side of Cherry Creek, but strong gusts sent sparks swirling and fanned the flames over the community on the east side of the creek.

Denver's fire crew barely slowed the spread of the blaze—even with the assistance of the town's citizens. Hundreds pitched in to help. Aside from the city ordinance stating citizens must do their part, there was also a tradition in the Old West that dictated everyone help fight a fire. Volunteers desperately chopped down wood structures that lay in the path of the fire, and they rescued goods from threatened buildings and stashed them in the sandy bottom of Cherry Creek.

The men who fought the fire were not prepared to deal with such an overwhelming inferno. In the absence of trained leadership, chaos ensued. Members of the fire department kept bumping into volunteers who weren't sure what they were supposed to be doing. While they tried to get organized and combat the blaze, flames fed on buildings of dry pine and were spread around by the wind. Soon whole blocks of the city were burning. Buckets of water thrown on the fire did nothing to slow it and most of the buildings on the east side of Cherry Creek were consumed by flames. The fire didn't stop until it had used up all available fuel. By daylight a four-block area in the middle of the business district lay in black and smoking ruins.

The Great Fire, as it came to be known in Denver, caused between $250,000 and $350,000 in damage. Seventy structures went up in smoke and 115 businesses were destroyed. Hundreds of people were left homeless. As important goods such as flour and sugar became scarce after the fire, their prices doubled. Fortunately—almost miraculously—no one was killed. The citizens of Denver were grateful for that, and they began rebuilding immediately, almost before the ashes cooled.

Several Denver companies were doing business within days of having their buildings burned to the ground. A man who'd lost his butcher shop raised a tent on his scorched property the day after the fire and was selling meat a few weeks later. Industrious boys wandered the burnt-out area in search of nails they could salvage and sell. Buildings were hauled across Cherry Creek and placed where businesses had burned. These lightweight wood structures provided temporary bases where business owners could get back on their feet; the structures were torn down and removed as soon as permanent buildings took their place. Local brick makers stepped up production and made huge profits. Durable building materials remained in high demand in Denver.

Few people had insurance, but there was local money available to finance the task of rebuilding. The Kountze brothers were viewed by many in Denver as heroes. Their bank had burned to the ground but they had the resources to build a new two-story brick bank—and to write loans for other local businesses to rebuild.

The fire had leveled a big chunk of the city but it didn't destroy Denver's spirit. In place of the hastily constructed wood buildings the fire had burned, solid and durable brick structures were raised. Two years after the Great Fire the red-brick buildings along the eastern side of Cherry Creek gave Denver's downtown an attractive and permanent look that pleased the city's civic boosters. Denver had risen from the ashes of the Great Fire.

THE GREAT FLOOD

- 1864 -

WILLIAM BYERS WALKED TOWARD THE EDGE of Denver City, wandering down street after street as he tried to figure out where to build the headquarters for his newspaper. When he reached Cherry Creek, a small stream with sandy beds lined by chokecherry bushes, he suddenly knew exactly where he should build: right in the middle of the creek. He would place his *Rocky Mountain News* office diplomatically between two rival towns—Denver City on one side of the creek, Auraria on the other. Sales of his newspaper wouldn't be limited in either place. Pleased by his brainstorm, Byers hurried through town, looking for someone who could sink piles into the bed of the creek and begin constructing his headquarters.

Indians and mountain men had warned gold seekers in Denver that the trickling waters of Cherry Creek could quickly turn into a raging torrent during times of heavy rain, but the settlers thought the mountain men were crazy, and they had no interest in the knowledge Native Americans had gleaned from living close to the land. Denver's citizens paid the waters of Cherry Creek little attention other than to use them as a source for panning gold. They put ramshackle buildings on the banks of Cherry Creek, and even built some structures on stilts in its bed.

The Arapaho and mountain men who saw people building in the middle of the stream scolded them, but the stubborn pioneers continued to build. Soon Cherry Creek was crammed with shacks and shanties and rickety buildings tottering on wooden stilts. Stores and offices straddled the creek. A Methodist church and a jail were constructed in the streambed. Even City Hall, in an effort to appear impartial between the feuding towns of Auraria and Denver City, followed the example of William Byers and built midstream on neutral ground. The dribbling creek alarmed none of the newcomers to the area. They noted that even in spring, when the mountain snowpack melted and rainstorms pummeled the plains, Cherry Creek rarely held more than a thin trickle of water. But this soon changed.

After Denver City and Auraria merged to become Denver, the *Rocky Mountain News* published the following when floodwaters rose along the Palmer Divide, a ridge jutting out from the Rocky Mountains southwest of Denver: "Cherry Creek appears to present a rather serious problem, for we have had a demonstration of what may be expected from a heavy rainfall on the Divide, though we are not yet inclined to believe the Indian claims that the whole settlement is subject to flood."

The debate over whether the flood danger was real or not was settled on the night of May 19, 1864. For an entire week leading up to that evening a heavy dumping of hail and rain had poured down on the mountains west of Denver. When the storm finally stopped on May 19, some citizens noticed that Cherry Creek was running higher than usual, but no one expressed concern. Other than the slowly rising waters, the coming flood gave little warning.

A few minutes before midnight, while some Denverites were in bed and others were in gambling halls, saloons, and brothels, a flash flood descended on the city. One man reported that he "heard a strange sound in the south like the noise of wind, which increased to a mighty roar as a great wall of water, bearing on its crest trees and other drift, rushed toward the settlement." The flood, which began in the upper end of the Cherry Creek watershed and in the Plum Creek drainage, reached its maximum height—some eyewitnesses said the crests of waves rose twenty feet or more—in Denver at about 2:00 A.M. on Friday, May 20. By 7:00 A.M. the waters had begun to lower. One frightened citizen of Denver described the flood this way: "It was the water engine of death dragging its destroying train of maddened waves, that defied the eye to number them, which was rushing down upon us." As the flood swept through town, moonlight and the bonfires of curious onlookers lit the destruction. Chaos ensued. "Alarm flew around, and all alike were ignorant of what to think, or say, or do, much less of knowing where to go with safety, or to save others."

Union soldiers from nearby Camp Weld built makeshift boats and navigated the rising waters, saving desperate citizens from drowning. Other concerned Denverites warned people away from the swelling stream as buildings in the bed of Cherry Creek and along its banks were smashed and swept away. The *Rocky Mountain News* headquarters was ruined; its printing press was destroyed. Printers who had worked late that night were sleeping in the building when the flood hit. They escaped by grabbing a rope thrown from shore. City Hall was devastated; its safe, containing town records and land ownership documents, was lost. The jail collapsed. One prisoner who had been freed by the flood only to find his life threatened by the rising tide grabbed hold of a passing cottonwood tree. He floated for miles downstream and was finally fished out of the swirling water. Records regarding the fate of prisoners set loose by the flood don't exist, but without a city hall to sentence them, or a jail to hold them, the liberated criminals likely went free.

Scores of businesses, churches, bridges, warehouses, stables, and outbuildings were borne away on the floodwaters. Ranches along the South Platte River were ruined. Both halves of Denver—the former Denver City on one side of Cherry Creek, Auraria on the other side—were joined in mutual destruction as several feet of water spread for miles in all directions, wiping out much of the fledgling frontier settlement. Between eight and nineteen people were reported killed by the flood, and estimates of the damage it caused, in 1864 dollars, range between $250,000 and $1,000,000. Countless citizens of Denver were left homeless and were forced to take temporary shelter in tents and wagons until new homes could be raised.

When the flood receded, it left in its wake a horrible stench from dead livestock, pools of contaminated water, acres of thick mud, and snarls and snags of debris. Fortunately, no major disease epidemics broke out. Unfortunately, however, food prices skyrocketed due to all the crops that had been destroyed and the livestock that had been killed on nearby farms and ranches.

Newspaperman William Byers not only lost the building where his paper was housed, he barely escaped the flood with his life. Water inundated his family's ranch house outside of town, picking it up and depositing it on a small island. An army colonel rescued the Byers family by boat. Byers almost immediately began setting up a new headquarters for his newspaper—but this time he located it on high, dry ground far from Cherry Creek. Soon the newspaper was printing and distributing copies throughout Denver.

Many other townspeople joined Byers and quickly rallied to begin the immense task of cleaning up and rebuilding their city. Because the area of Auraria to the west of Cherry Creek lay lower than the original Denver City to the east, Auraria had suffered more destruction. Owners of businesses that had been ruined in Auraria rebuilt on the east side of Cherry Creek, lessening the rivalry between the east and west sides of Denver. The creek that had once divided the city now united it.

THE SAND CREEK MASSACRE

- 1864 -

As COLONEL CHIVINGTON ASSEMBLED HIS MEN in the chilly dawn on a lonesome stretch of prairie southeast of Denver, he ran his fingers along the barrel of his rifle. He told himself he was doing God's work. His troops blew on their hands and kicked their toes around inside their boots trying to stay warm. Below them on the plain, a group of Native Americans slept under buffalo blankets, unaware of the danger at hand.

In 1864 Colorado Governor John Evans, in response to increasing hostilities with the Native Americans in the region, was granted permission by Washington to raise a Colorado regiment with the purpose of defeating those Arapaho and Cheyenne who had been raiding ranches and attacking stagecoaches and supply lines around Denver. When a white family was murdered and mutilated by Arapahos near town, many Denverites tried to goad the Governor into immediately launching an all-out war against Indians.

To lead the Colorado regiment Governor Evans selected John Chivington, a tall and burly Civil War hero who had distinguished himself in the Battle of Glorieta Pass. Nicknamed the "Fighting Parson," Chivington was also a preacher who had organized the first Methodist Sunday School in Denver and who had spoken out passionately against slavery. Chivington saw the battle with Native Americans as a "holy war" and called Indians "heathen savages." He was not alone in his ideas. The *Rocky Mountain News* stated, "The tribes by which we are surrounded are our inferiors physically, morally, mentally."

By the time Chivington's Third Colorado Regiment (mustered from a pool of laborers from Denver and miners from the mountains), was patrolling the South Platte River, the Indians in the area had stopped their attacks. Chivington's Third Regiment soon earned the label "bloodless" by a Denver citizenry still reeling from Indian raids on white outlying settlements.

While Chivington's Third Regiment went about its uneventful business on the South Platte, Cheyenne and Arapaho leaders came to Denver to ask for peace. "What shall I do with the Third Regiment if I make peace?" Governor Evans was reported to ask Major Edward Wynkoop, who supported the Indians' plan for nonviolent coexistence with white settlers. The Arapaho and Cheyenne leaders pleading for peace were sent to Fort Lyon, where they were fed by the kind Wynkoop. But Major Wynkoop was soon replaced by another army major, who not only stopped feeding the Native Americans but also told them to leave Fort Lyon and set up camp at Sand Creek to the north. The U.S. Army promised them sanctuary there. Those Cheyenne and Arapaho who agreed to settle at Sand Creek posted no guards and had no reason to believe they wouldn't be safe.

The *Rocky Mountain News* editorialized, "Shall we not go for them, their lodges, squaws, and all? [We support] a few months of active extermination against the red devils." Encouraged by a majority of Denver's citizens, and with at least the tacit—and perhaps even the explicit—approval of Governor Evans, Chivington and several hundred United States soldiers of the Third Colorado Regiment left Denver for Fort Lyon. From there, in the early morning of November 29, 1864, five days after Thanksgiving, they marched to Sand Creek and Chivington gave his men this pep talk, "I don't tell you to kill all ages and sex[es], but look back on the plains of the Platte, where your mothers, fathers, brothers, sisters have been slain, and their blood saturating the sands of the Platte."

At daybreak Chivington's men surprised the sleeping people in camp. Chief Black Kettle of the Cheyenne raised an American flag to show his people's allegiance with the United States Government, as well as a white flag to signal their desire for peace. Despite the chief's attempts, and despite the efforts by many others in the camp to surrender, no prisoners were taken by the Third Regiment. Chivington said, "I have come to kill Indians and believe it is right and honorable to use any means under God's heaven to kill Indians."

As howitzers were moved into position on a hilltop overlooking the camp, fierce fighting erupted. Women, children, teenagers, and the elderly were gunned down, beaten to death, scalped, and mutilated by Chivington and his soldiers. Fingers and ears were chopped off as trophies. Some of the Cheyenne and Arapaho dug into sandy cliffs along the creek in a desperate effort to escape the bullets spitting from the howitzers. Some dove into the creek's icy waters and tried to hide under the banks.

A few United States soldiers, including Captain Silas Soule, refused to join the attack. "It looked too hard for me to see little children on their knees begging for their lives, have their brains beat out like dogs," he said. Nevertheless, the killing continued, by some estimates for eight hours. After United States soldiers finished shredding teepees with the howitzers, they trained the big guns on the cliffs and the creek. Some fast Indian warriors managed to run away from the battleground and flee the slaughter. Most accounts of the massacre place the number of dead Cheyenne and Arapaho at 163—though some estimates range as high as 500.

After the smoke cleared from the battleground, the *Rocky Mountain News* quickly reported the "battle" at Sand Creek in the following way: "All acquitted themselves well, and Colorado soldiers once again covered themselves with glory." Chivington, boasting that he'd killed between four and five hundred Indians at Sand Creek, was hailed as a hero when he returned to Denver. A holiday was declared and hundreds lined the streets as Chivington's troops paraded through town. In a Denver theater Chivington showed scalps from people he and his men had slaughtered at Sand Creek. The audience greeted this grisly display with a standing ovation.

Chivington felt confident that his heroism would help him launch a successful political career. However, some Denverites who had worked for a peaceful solution to the conflict, or who had witnessed Chivington's butchery first hand, immediately spoke out against him. Congress started making inquiries as word of Chivington's misconduct at Sand Creek spread. After poring over hundreds of pages of testimony, Congress declared that Colonel Chivington had disgraced his office and his country by leading a "foul and dastardly massacre." They immediately ordered a court martial. While the United States Army investigated the incident at Sand Creek, Denver was placed under martial law. The inquiries ended Chivington's military career and put a stop to his political ambitions, but he was never punished by the army or by Congress. Almost all modern accounts of the massacre describe Chivington as a cold-blooded killer of innocent people.

Denver tried to forget the blood that had been shed at its doorstep, but for the Cheyenne and Arapaho, the wound was too raw. Immediately following the massacre, some tribal members in the Denver area joined the Dog Soldiers, a group of fierce Cheyenne fighters who had devoted their lives to making war with the United States. "Now no peace," one prominent Indian leader was quoted as saying after the massacre. Soon corrals, barns, and wagons of white settlers near Denver lay in smoking ruins. Stage stops and telegraph stations on the plains east of Denver were attacked relentlessly until no mail, food, or communication could reach the town. For several weeks, food prices in Denver skyrocketed, and the town was gripped by fear.

Some Arapaho and Cheyenne leaders, such as Chief Little Raven, continued to work toward nonviolent coexistence with white Denverites, but all the Arapaho and Cheyenne people who had survived Sand Creek—regardless of whether they wanted peace or war—were soon forced out of Colorado and relocated on reservations in Oklahoma and Wyoming. Chief Black Kettle, who had tried so hard to achieve peace, escaped Sand Creek unharmed but was killed by Lieutenant Colonel George Armstrong Custer's men in Oklahoma almost four years to the day after the Sand Creek massacre. Sand Creek set off years of bloody warfare across the Great Plains and it is often cited as an important cause of the Battle of the Little Big Horn, in which Cheyenne warriors in Montana killed to the last man a United States cavalry detachment commanded by Custer.

Though Sand Creek was not the first, or the last, or the bloodiest massacre of Native Americans by United States troops, it became a powerful symbol of the cruelty toward the original owners of the land that whites occupied, often by force, as they expanded westward. Sand Creek changed how the nation thought about American Indians, and it is often used as an example of how Native Americans were mistreated by whites. In 2000 Congress established Sand Creek as an official historic site in order to "recognize the national significance of the massacre in American history, and its ongoing significance to the Cheyenne and Arapahoe people and the descendants of the massacre victims." On August 2, 2005, President George W. Bush gave final approval, and now the National Park Service is creating the country's first historic site dedicated solely to a massacre.

A RACE TO BUILD A RAILROAD

- 1870 -

MORE THAN ONE THOUSAND PEOPLE GATHERED IN DENVER beneath a bright afternoon sun. The air was electric with optimism. Beer was served; a band played. Two elegantly dressed ladies guided a ceremonial plow that cut into the prairie, marking the spot where men and mules were to lay the rails that would end Denver's isolation.

Denver lay in the middle of nowhere. One early observer described Denver's strange and isolated location, saying the city "looked just as if it had been dropped out of the clouds accidentally, by someone who meant to carry it further on, but got tired, and let it fall anywhere." Indeed, Denver was an island of civilization amid the vast sea of the high plains, linked to the rest of the country by a weeklong journey of jolting stagecoach travel through dangerous territory. If Denver were ever to emerge from the wilderness as an important city, it had to be linked to other cities by a means of transportation swifter and safer than the stage line. For Denver to grow, it had to join the rest of the country by rail.

Denverites were confident that the Union Pacific Railroad would route its line through their city as it moved westward through the Rockies toward completion of the transcontinental railroad. Denver's leading rival, the small town of Golden at the base of the Rockies, had other ideas. Town boosters in Golden mounted an all-out campaign to attract the transcontinental railroad and become Colorado's central transportation hub. They organized the Colorado Central Railroad, and the race was on to link to the transcontinental line.

Clever propagandists in Denver told Union Pacific officials that the Rocky Mountains to the west of the city weren't really mountains—they were just hills that could be easily traveled. A Union Pacific engineer who surveyed a possible rail route through Berthoud Pass and was nearly buried by a blizzard didn't agree. He told the railroad that a route north of Denver through Wyoming would be much faster, cheaper, and safer to build. The Union Pacific took his advice. It bypassed Denver in favor of Cheyenne, Wyoming, and its gentler terrain with rolling hills that really were hills—not jagged, snow-clad Rocky Mountain summits like the ones near Denver.

Though the decision of the Union Pacific was perfectly logical, the hopes of Denverites for "capturing the iron horse" were dashed. Businessmen and investors left Denver in droves for Cheyenne, assuming the small Wyoming town would boom and grow into a major supply center and an important city while Denver would fade into obscurity. The *Cheyenne Daily Leader* rubbed salt in the wound by writing, "Denver is too near Cheyenne to ever amount to much."

Some stubborn Denver supporters, however, ignored those who said their town was destined to die. They stayed and kept fighting to bring the iron horse to town. While they went to work trying to convince the Union Pacific to build a 106-mile branchline from Cheyenne to Denver, the Kansas Pacific announced that it would build a line to Denver, linking it to the East. Denverites were elated—until the Kansas Pacific got into financial trouble and said the railway could only be built if Denver quickly raised $2 million to fund its construction. As if this weren't bad enough news, Denver received word that Golden had already begun grading its own rail line to Cheyenne and was well on its way to linking itself to the transcontinental railroad. Denver, it seemed, was losing the race.

But Denver didn't give up. Civic leaders, with little in common, shared a vision: They saw Denver not as a sleepy frontier outpost but as a major metropolis and the economic powerhouse of the Rockies. In addition to this vision, they shared a love of challenges and the thrill of building something new. They had left their old lives in the East and had come to the mountains and plains of the West to reinvent themselves; by creating a thriving city where there was just a dusty hamlet they would do exactly that. So they pooled their collective will and hard work, taking on the monumental task of building a railroad themselves.

Town leaders organized a meeting and encouraged every citizen of Denver to attend. At the meeting, the Denver Board of Trade was organized, and the Board quickly incorporated the Denver Pacific Railroad and Telegraph Company and persuaded voters to approve bond support for constructing the Denver Pacific Railroad. Business leaders were encouraged to invest heavily in the company; ordinary citizens were asked to buy what stock they could and to donate their labor. Three hundred thousand dollars was raised in three days. Many townsfolk agreed to help grade the railbed and to chop trees in the mountains and then float the logs down various rivers to the plains below where they could be made into railroad ties.

Denver declared a holiday for the Denver Pacific groundbreaking. While Denverites labored feverishly on the prairie to build the railroad, town boosters lobbied people with power in Washington, trying to convince congressmen to assist them in their efforts. Their badgering was rewarded: Congress agreed to donate nine hundred thousand acres of land for the railroad right-of-way, which allowed the Denver Pacific to secure loans.

On the afternoon of June 15, directors of the Denver Pacific gathered on the rooftop of the First National Bank and with the aid of a telescope they watched smoke from the construction train as it chugged toward town. Tracks reached the city limits four days later. The frantic scramble and hard work paid off when the rail line joining Denver to the transcontinental railroad in Cheyenne was completed before Golden had a chance to finish its line. Denver had won the race to become the central transportation hub of Colorado. The dream of a group of relentless and enterprising optimists finally became a reality as the iron horse roared through town in June of 1870.

Silver spikes, symbolic of railroad prosperity, were traditionally driven into the last piece of rail to complete a line. But when Denver's final spike was hammered in by one of the men who'd built the railroad, it was made of ordinary iron. Miners who had transported a genuine silver spike from a mine in the Rockies had, according to rumor, paid a bar tab with the valuable spike. True to form, Denverites improvised and made the best of a bad situation. They wrapped a regular iron spike in shiny white paper so it looked like silver. Few in the crowd of ecstatic onlookers knew the difference.

The arrival of the railroad in 1870 marked what has been called "the proudest year in the whole history of Denver." Population and business tripled during the following three years. After the first railroad arrived, boomtown Denver quickly built a steel spiderweb of rails to profit from the Rocky Mountain region's mining, farming, and ranching riches. Denver's economy galloped ahead of its competitors. The city became, as its ambitious boosters had always hoped it would be, the rail hub of the Rockies and an industrial powerhouse on the high plains. The enormous rail network enabled Denver to establish its dominance. As Denver grew, Cheyenne and Golden diminished in importance. With the help of the iron horse, Denver had outraced its rivals. Gold and silver ores mined in the mountains rode the rails to Denver's smelters, which employed thousands. A hundred trains or more a day steamed in and out of Denver's Union Station, and black clouds of smelter smoke hung over the city signaling that Denver had become a city to be reckoned with.

THE HOP STREET RIOT

- 1880 -

DAVE COOK, PREVIOUSLY DENVER'S CITY MARSHAL and now head of a special branch of the Denver police force known as the Rocky Mountain Detectives, was awakened by screaming and angry shouts on the street outside. But before he could run out to investigate, his phone rang. It was the mayor of Denver. He sounded desperate. He needed Cook's help.

In the early days of Denver, opium use may not have been as socially acceptable as drunkenness, but many of the town's citizens still got "hopped up" in opium dens clustered next to Denver's red-light district in an area known as Hop Alley, or Hop Street. Populated largely by Chinese immigrants, Hop Alley, along present-day Wazee, was the scene of the only major race riot in Denver's history.

After the completion of the transcontinental railroad, the Chinese laborers who had worked on the railroad soon found themselves without jobs in a foreign land. Many of them migrated to Colorado mines and railroad towns in search of work. They were often run out of rural settlements. Most of the Chinese who remained in Colorado moved to Denver, a bustling city where they had a better chance of finding employment and making lives for themselves.

Despite the efforts of many Denverites to make the Chinese feel unwelcome, from the time the last spike was driven into the transcontinental railroad in 1869 until 1880, between 250 and 500 Chinese immigrants settled in Denver, almost all of them around Hop Street. For several months leading up to October 31, 1880, Denver's newspapers ignited public anger against the Chinese by printing inflammatory editorials blaming them for starving white workmen, encouraging prostitution, and spreading the evil of opium smoking. Newspaper articles also labeled them as "Celestial heathens" for their religious beliefs and practices. Economic insecurity and religious intolerance mixed together in a wicked brew that was stirred daily by the papers. Politicians played on this city-wide hysteria by making anti-Chinese sentiment the central theme of their campaigns. It seemed that violence might eventually be unavoidable.

When a fistfight in a pool hall on Hop Street broke out between a Chinese man and a white man, other whites jumped into the fray. Soon a mob had gathered and was shouting slogans such as, "Stamp out the yellow plague!" and, "The Chinese must go!" The melee quickly spread up and down Hop Street. Chinese businesses were looted and vandalized and Chinese homes were burned to the ground. Denver's police force, which consisted of a mere fifteen members and lacked a chief, failed to restore order. Denver's mayor dispatched the fire department, which sprayed the rioters with their hoses. But even this dousing didn't put an end to what the city leaders and newspapers had started. The violence began at noon and lasted until midnight, when Dave Cook and his Rocky Mountain Detectives were finally called in.

Cook gathered fifteen men from his detective agency and then rounded up a selection of other tough gunfighters. By this time three thousand rioters were running amuck on Hop Street. Cook and his men arrested nine thugs who were trying to torch a building. When the angry crowd attempted to free these prisoners, Cook instructed his men to fire at the ground and then aim the smoking muzzles of their guns at the faces of the rioters. Cook's ploy worked; the mob backed off. Led by Cook and his crew, police forces finally quieted the city.

Before Cook could stop the violence, however, dozens of terrified Chinese had been beaten by rioters and one man was killed. On Seventeenth Street, a mob of Denverites smashed windows in laundries where Hop Street's residents worked. Then they surrounded Sing Lee. In his seventies or eighties and clad in a black silk shirt and white pants, his only crime was not being able to run away and escape. The mob fitted one end of a rope around his neck, threw the other end over the cross arm of a telegraph pole, and began to pull. The old man, his legs kicking, was lifted into the air.

Some historians have claimed that the cause of the riot was a disagreement between a Chinese laundryman and his customer, and others have argued that the victim was Look Young, a twenty-eight-year-old man who was beaten to death. Regardless of the exact flashpoint that started the riot, and regardless of the victim's identity, there is no dispute over the fact that a Chinese man was brutally murdered by the mob.

Scores of Denver's citizens joined in the melee but some compassionate Denverites took Chinese people into their homes during the riot to protect them. Several residents showed remarkable courage; saloon keeper James Veatch sheltered refugees at great danger to himself. Gambler Jim Moon leveled a revolver at rioters, backing them away from a Chinese man. A group of prostitutes led by

Madam Lizzie Preston offered sanctuary in their bordello to thirty-four persecuted Chinese; the ladies armed themselves with champagne bottles and high-heeled shoes to hold the murderous mob at bay.

Nearly two hundred Chinese citizens were placed in Denver's jails for "safekeeping"; four days later they were allowed to return to the ruins of their neighborhood. Every Chinese house, with maybe one or two exceptions, had been destroyed. According to the *Rocky Mountain News,* Hop Street was "gutted as completely as though a cyclone had come in one door and passed . . . out the rear. There was nothing left . . . whole, and the rooms, so recently the abode of ignorance, vice, and shame, contained nothing beyond the horrid stench emitted by the little wads of opium." Four men were arrested for the lynching but were later acquitted.

Though the Chinese did not bear the sole brunt of Denver's ethnic hatred, and prejudice was suffered by groups ranging from Native Americans to African Americans, from Italians to Germans, the Chinese were the only group to be the focus of a major riot.

Following the riot, the numbers of Chinese in Denver increased as they rebuilt their businesses and established neighborhoods beyond Hop Street. Many tried to blend with western culture by changing the way they dressed and abandoning their traditional customs and beliefs. Nevertheless, the *Rocky Mountain News* continued to proclaim that "the Chinese must go," and Colorado's Bureau of Labor Statistics reported that if the Chinese were to disappear in Denver, as many as one thousand laundry jobs would be freed up for white laborers. As public attacks such as these stirred up anger among white Denverites, many in the Chinese community, fearing a repeat of the Hop Street Riot, fled Colorado.

BUILDING A HOUSE OF MIRRORS

1889

As Mattie Silks watched miners newly rich from the mountains stumble out of Denver's saloons, she fingered the diamond-cross pendant she always wore in public. She smiled to herself, knowing that she'd found the perfect place to ply her trade. Now she needed the perfect building. It was time to abandon the tent-based traveling bordello she had taken from one rowdy mountain town to another and establish something more permanent.

Denver's first prostitutes were Native-American women in teepees on the edge of town along Cherry Creek, an area that became known as "Indian Row." The first non–Native-American prostitute was a nineteen-year-old former wife of a minister. Soon prostitutes with names such as Lily the Fox, Mormon Ann, Hook and Ladder Kate, Cockeyed Liz, Red Stockings, and Liver-Lip Lou were filling Denver's streets and gambling halls.

A red-light district developed south of Cherry Creek along McGaa Street (later renamed Holladay Street in order to purge the city of memories of William McGaa, one of the original founders of Denver and a drunkard who'd lived with multiple Indian brides). When the pleasure houses along Holladay Street became brazen enough to display prostitutes in their windows and to hang signs with sayings such as "Men Taken In And Done For," the city, out of respect for the pioneer stage line owner Ben Holladay for whom the street had been named, again renamed it. This time, perhaps with a wink and a smile by the town council, it was officially renamed Market Street. Unofficially, people throughout the West began to refer to it as "the wickedest street in the Rockies."

So woven into the fabric of Denver was prostitution that both the *Republican* and the *Rocky Mountain News* reported that the city council had failed to conduct any business in one of its meetings because a quorum had not been present; the men who had failed to turn up had instead chosen to attend "the opening of a new and fashionable den of prostitution on Holladay St."

When madams from mining camps and from the East got word of Denver's accepting attitude toward prostitution, they flocked to the area. A section of parlor houses known as "The Row" filled up with more than one thousand prostitutes, spreading from Market Street out to three downtown city blocks.

Street prostitutes serviced customers in cribs: small, filthy houses where ruthless madams collected the majority of the money their prostitutes earned. They typically gave the women little rest and little food, and turned them out into the streets with no help when they became sick or pregnant. Some of the first brothels were simply rickety log cabins on well-worn dirt streets. As business boomed, brothels of more permanent and elegant construction were erected. Many of the houses of ill-fame lining Market Street were clean and stylish—and pricey for the men who visited them.

Jennie Rogers built the most impressive house of all. Six feet tall, hot tempered, and never seen in public without her emerald earrings, Rogers showed up on Market Street just after Mattie Silks. Rogers blackmailed businessmen in Denver by threatening to expose their dealings with prostitutes. She harassed one prominent businessman by spreading rumors about the disappearance of his first wife. She even went so far as to bury a skull in his backyard; then she had a police chief who was her lover "discover" the skull and threaten the man with prosecution if he didn't give Rogers money. She used the funds to build The House of Mirrors, a ritzy two-story building designed by architect William Quayle (who also designed Denver's First Congregational Church). After The House of Mirrors opened its doors in 1889, it quickly became the most popular parlor house on Market Street, and was soon known as "the plushest whorehouse from the Missouri River to the West Coast" and "the swankiest parlor house between Kansas City and San Francisco."

The House of Mirrors aroused the envy of Rogers's friend and competitor, Mattie Silks, who soon bought the house from Rogers and ran it herself. The House of Mirrors boasted sixteen bedrooms, a ballroom, and four parlors graced with ornate woodwork, crystal chandeliers, lace curtains, oriental rugs, and, in the front parlor, mirrored ceilings and walls.

A practice started by Rogers—and continued by Silks when she took over The House of Mirrors—was to select only the women she deemed the most beautiful and personable to work for her. Rogers, and later Silks, insisted on good grooming. Their "brides of the multitudes" were well fed and finely attired. They had to buy their own wigs and dresses, however, which cut significantly into their earnings.

In addition to their hundreds of prostitutes, Silks and Rogers also hired for the House of Mirrors a number of bouncers, chefs, kitchen help, piano players, bartenders, and croupiers. It could even be said that they hired police; routine payments were made to law enforcers to look the other way while business was conducted. Regular graft payments and widespread corruption among police and politicians ensured that prostitution remained one of Denver's most viable industries. Many of the police and politicians were, of course, regulars in Denver's most infamous house. Though repeatedly warned by physicians of syphilis and gonorrhea epidemics, local authorities paid little more than lip service to the health concerns, making a few public statements about ridding the city of prostitution but doing little to actually curb it. The House of Mirrors did a brisk business for more than two decades before moral reform finally swept through the city and dimmed the red lights of The Row.

Jennie Rogers and Mattie Silks are both buried in Denver's prestigious Fairmont Cemetery—near, it has been said, many of their former clients. The House of Mirrors still stands at 1942 Market Street in downtown Denver. After serving as a Buddhist temple for a time, the building was restored. It is now a museum, restaurant, and bar that groups can book for weddings and other special occasions.

The bust of Madam Rogers crowns the house's pediment. Carved into the façade below her are the busts of the businessmen she blackmailed to build the Denver parlor house that later became the centerpiece of a thriving industry under the watchful eye of Madam Mattie Silks. Mattie's House of Mirrors today exists at the center of another thriving Denver industry, one perhaps even more profitable than prostitution: tourism.

THE SILVER PANIC

- 1893 -

GOVERNOR WAITE PACED AROUND THE OFFICE, his fingers working through his bushy beard. He stopped in front of a window and looked out to the Capitol lawn where a small army of unemployed men was shouting at anyone who would listen. They were claiming that unless their families were given some immediate help, they would starve to death. The Governor hated to see their suffering, and he hated the deplorable state that Denver had fallen into. These desperate times called for drastic measures. A plan started to brew in the governor's head. He knew what he needed to do.

After the federal government agreed to buy silver to back the value of United States currency in 1890, silver mining soon eclipsed gold mining as Colorado's leading industry. Denver's prosperity depended on supplying the silver mines in the mountains, refining ore in the city's smelters, and transporting the refined metal back east by rail. But as the nation's economy headed south and the price of silver began to plummet, the federal government dropped a bombshell on Denver: It announced that it would stop purchasing silver. The bottom quickly fell out of the market. The price of silver sank so low that the mines and smelters, unable to operate at a profit, shut down, putting an abrupt end to Denver's silver bonanza and throwing thousands out of work.

Both of Denver's senators headed to Washington to address a special session of Congress. They tried desperately to convince federal lawmakers to continue buying silver to back United States currency. Congress, however, decided to maintain a gold standard only—they would purchase no more silver from Colorado mines. The senators returned to Denver distraught.

Denver's collapsing economy frightened hordes of the city's panicked citizens into withdrawing their money. Overwhelmed by the sudden drain of funds, a dozen of Denver's biggest banks closed their doors. Because there was no federal bank insurance, people with accounts who didn't withdraw their savings in time from the failing institutions lost everything.

The young city fell swiftly from shining optimism to deep depression. Riches-to-rags stories abounded. The builder of the Brown Palace, for example, after tapping his enormous silver-mining fortune to build the elaborate hotel and donating the land where the state capitol building was constructed, lost everything and had to hole up in one of his own hotel rooms to hide from creditors. While they pounded on his door and tried to evict him, he was saved at the last minute by a friend who bought the mortgage to the hotel.

The Silver Panic also erased the vast fortune of Denver's "Silver King," Horace Tabor, the once-wealthy financer of the Tabor Grand Opera House. Almost overnight Tabor traded a life of fabulous opulence (in which he could afford a $75,000 necklace for his bride and diamond rings for his young daughters) for the modest salary of a postmaster job—one he was lucky to have as the unemployment rate in Denver soared.

The Silver Panic swept the entire nation, but it hit Denver particularly hard. Thousands of out-of-work miners drifted down from the mountains seeking jobs. Businesses failed, mortgages were foreclosed on, and real estate values plunged. Hungry families begged in the streets. Raggedy towns made of tents and makeshift shacks sprang up along the South Platte.

Denver at first provided tents and food to out-of-work people but soon the city grew overwhelmed by the demand. On Governor Waite's dubious watch, a scheme was developed to rid the area of unemployed drifters: It gave them free lumber so they could build flatboats and float away from Denver. Some men died attempting to navigate the swirling currents and hidden sandbars of the South Platte. Railroads aided Denver's efforts to rid itself of the unemployed by dropping their fares out of town. A group of desperate men who couldn't afford even these new meager fares hijacked a Union Pacific train and forced the crew to transport them for free.

Crime and suicides became rampant among Denver's desperate citizens. As the economy tumbled ever downward, hostility toward Denver's recent immigrants increased and the city's murder rate skyrocketed. An angry mob of drifters stormed a jail where an Italian bartender was being held for allegedly killing a customer. Chanting ethnic slurs, the mob rioted, ripping up streetcar rails outside the jail and then kicking down the door. As thousands of Denver's citizens looked on and did nothing, a lynchmob dragged the bartender outside. They hung him from the nearest cottonwood tree and filled his body with bullets. Bloodstained branches of the tree where he'd been hung were sold in the street as souvenirs.

While Denver descended into Silver Panic chaos, Governor Waite thought it might be a good time to rid the city of sin. With its history of rampant gambling, prostitution, and saloon keeping, he and many of Colorado's citizens in rural towns thought of Denver as a den of iniquity. But his timing to purge the city of its vices was highly questionable, as were his methods.

Waite tried to remove from office those police and fire commissioners he thought were protecting Denver's gambling and prostitution industries. The officials he went after barricaded themselves in the Denver City Hall. Policemen, firemen, and criminal cronies armed with guns and dynamite rallied around them, guarding city hall from the windows and rooftops of nearby buildings. Waite ordered state troops to march on city hall to bring the corrupt commissioners to justice. Inside city hall, the commissioners and their cronies prepared bombs to throw at the four hundred militiamen assembled outside. These militiamen were meanwhile readying their artillery, including two Gatling guns. As the situation veered between comedy and tragedy, curious Denverites crowded the streets to watch how it would play out.

But before anyone fired a shot, the Colorado State Supreme Court avoided disaster by ruling that the governor *did* have the right to replace commissioners, but *did not* have the authority to use the Colorado Infantry to do it for him. The court's intervention put a stop to the madness and restored some semblance of sanity to the city. The commissioners surrendered peacefully and left office when instructed to do so by the court.

The Silver Panic and all the mayhem associated with it subsided when a gold bonanza at Cripple Creek in the first years of the twentieth century once again sent Colorado's economy booming. Denver rebounded but Governor Waite did not: he was punished at the polls in the next election by voters who thought his radical schemes had only served to worsen the Silver Panic.

THE GREAT BLIZZARD

- 1913 -

Streetcar operator Oscar Klein had seen some Colorado blizzards, but none of them had prepared him for the storm of December 1913. To this day it still ranks as the biggest snowstorm in Denver's recorded history.

It began on a Monday. Just another weather front on the high plains. A few scattered flakes drifted down from the dark sky. "It kept going Tuesday and Wednesday but was still pretty light," Oscar recalled. "Then, on Thursday afternoon, it really wound up and, by evening, everything in town was stopped."

Oscar kept trying to navigate his streetcar along rails drifted over with snow until the car stalled on Thirteenth Avenue near Broadway. It stayed there for three days. Men on snowshoes brought food, water, and supplies to Oscar and other stranded streetcar operators and passengers.

Weather records describe the early phases of the storm that began on December 1 as moderate and not at all unusual for a Colorado snowstorm. By the end of the third day, eight inches of snow lay on the ground—not an alarming amount, and many in Denver assumed the storm was over. However, according to meteorological experts, on Thursday, December 4, "all hell broke loose." Heavy snow developed along the Front Range and the blizzard continued through Friday. It finally moved east to Kansas on Saturday, December 6.

By the end of the blizzard, areas along Denver's present-day I–25 corridor were reporting three to four feet of snow. The blizzard blanketed the entire Front Range of the Rockies in an area stretching from Trinidad in the south of Colorado to Cheyenne, Wyoming, in the north. The storm's heaviest snowfall was to the west of Denver in Georgetown, which received a whopping seven feet two inches!

Not only did a lot of heavy, wet snow fall, but it was blown by strong winds into drifts up to twenty feet tall. Transportation ceased and businesses throughout Denver shut down for days. Thousands of stranded people who couldn't return to their homes crammed into auditoriums and other public buildings. The roofs of houses and businesses throughout the city collapsed from the weight of the wet snow. Several people went missing in the storm and its aftermath.

People throughout Denver pitched in to help fellow citizens. The Tramway Company sent a brigade of four thousand men armed with shovels out into the streets. Students from the Colorado School of Mines in Golden, just west of Denver, dug nonstop for three days to rescue eight people stranded in a streetcar. People on snowshoes delivered much-needed supplies to hospitals. People on horseback delivered the mail.

The St. Clara Orphanage was rescued by elephants. During the blizzard, the orphanage ran out of coal and the children who lived there were faced with freezing temperatures. The publishers of the publicity-hungry *Denver Post,* whether from kindness or from the attention they knew their act would earn them, sent wagonloads of coal to the orphanage. Struggling along a street that passed by circus grounds, the horses of the coal teams got stuck in deep drifts. The wagons wouldn't budge but the resourceful drivers didn't give up. They left the carts and waded through the snow to the circus, where they asked to use elephants. The elephants wrapped their trunks around the rear axles of the buried carts and lifted. The horses pulled the freed wagons the rest of the way to the orphanage, delivering the valuable cargo of coal and saving the orphans from the cold.

Elsewhere in the city, more carefree children and adults, free of work and school, strapped on snowshoes and stepped out of second-story windows to build snowmen, excavate tunnels, and hurl snowballs. When the sun came out and melted the forts and collapsed the tunnels, Denver's streets were filled with floodwaters, creating a soggy mess that had to be cleaned up by work crews. Men were paid $2.50 per day to shovel wet snow into wagons. Houses with roofs that had survived the weight of the snow were flooded with water when the snow began to melt. Some of the deepest drifts didn't completely disappear until summer.

When statisticians tallied up the effects of the Great Blizzard of 1913 they determined that the five-day storm had dumped a record total of over forty-seven inches on Denver, the most snow ever recorded in a single Denver snowstorm. More than twenty million tons of snow had buried the city, crushing at least fourteen buildings. The storm definitely caused deaths, but reports vary as to exactly how many. Some tallies go as high as thirty-four.

The blizzard did have some positive effects. Many of Colorado's strict building codes today are a direct result of all the collapses caused by the heavy snows; contemporary structures are designed to withstand a storm as fierce as the Great Blizzard of 1913. In addition, the plains of eastern Colorado received an extraordinary amount of moisture from the snow dump and the rain that preceded it—the most December precipitation for that area in recorded history. Wheat grew tall and cattle fattened on the greened plains the following spring.

Weather researchers in Denver today analyze the Great Blizzard of 1913 not only to create a historical record of the past event, but also to help the city prepare for epic snowstorms of the future. Meteorologists say it isn't a question of *if* a blizzard as big as the one that pounded Denver in 1913 will strike the city again—it's a question of when.

On December 24, 1982, a Christmas storm brought Denver to a standstill with nearly three feet of snow. On October 25, 1997, a blizzard dumped twenty-one inches of snow in forty-eight hours, causing a power outage that lasted three days. After a snowstorm on the first day of spring in 2003 pounded the city and buried some foothill locations west of Denver beneath six feet of white, some dubbed it the "Blizzard of the Century." True, but there are still many years left in this most recent century, and chances are good that Denver will get hit with a bigger snowstorm—perhaps one even bigger than the Great Blizzard of 1913—before this century ends. Thanks to the lessons learned in 1913, buildings in Denver will withstand the weight of snow when the next great winter storm buries the town, and farmers on the plains surrounding the city will be ready to reap a bountiful harvest when the drifts melt away in spring.

THE EPIDEMIC

- 1918 -

KATHERINE ANNE PORTER'S FEVER ROSE SO HIGH her hair turned white and fell from her head. As she writhed in bed, sweat dripped from her boiling skin. Hallucinations paraded through her fevered mind as her landlady stood outside her bedroom door shouting about "the plague."

The disease that appeared in Denver in the fall of 1918 was spreading fast, but doctors had not yet realized how swiftly it could reach epidemic proportions. In 1918 World War I was ending and peace was near. Yet hundreds of thousands of Americans died that year, and they weren't casualties of the war. Between 1918 and 1920, forty to one hundred million people worldwide were killed by the influenza virus known as "Spanish flu" (due to the mistaken belief that it had originated in Spain). An estimated 675,000 of those deaths occurred in the United States, where the deadly virus took ten times as many American lives as did World War I. Of the American soldiers who died in the European war theater, as many as half were slain not by bullets or bombs but by the flu. Far more deadly than the German army, Spanish flu spread with terrifying speed through both the military and civilian populations. The World Health Organization has called the 1918 influenza epidemic "the most deadly disease event in the history of humanity." It killed more people even than the "Black Death," the bubonic plague of the Middle Ages.

To the terrified citizens of Denver the flu indeed seemed like some sort of medieval plague. The onset of illness was typically sudden. In a matter of a few hours people could go from good health to being so weak they couldn't walk. Victims complained of severe aches in their muscles, backs, joints, and heads. With fevers rising up to 105 degrees, the sick were visited by wild bouts of delirium.

Pulitzer Prize winning writer Katherine Anne Porter witnessed the epidemic after moving to Denver. She'd been divorced and wanted to begin a new life in a new place. After landing a reporting job for the *Rocky Mountain News,* Porter contracted the disease and became deathly ill. She barely survived. After recovering, she watched the man who had nursed her back to health die. Porter's *Pale Horse, Pale Rider,* set in Denver during the influenza epidemic, describes the devastating effects of the disease in the frenzied dreamlike imagery of a feverish hallucination: "All the theaters and nearly all of the shops and restaurants are closed, and the streets have been full of funerals all day and ambulances all night." Porter gave an interview when *Pale Horse, Pale Rider* was being made into a film for television. Asked about her sources, she replied, "It's a true story. . . . It seems to me true that I died then, I died once, and I never have feared death since."

The virus did not discriminate between famous writer or anonymous foot soldier, and it hit the young and otherwise healthy particularly hard. Some who caught the Spanish flu simply suffered from the fever, cough, and aches that usually accompany a mild bout of flu. Others, however, had symptoms that proved fatal: high fever, chills, vomiting, delirium—even blood spurting from the eyes and ears. Autopsies on patients who died within forty-eight hours of contracting the disease revealed lungs so heavy with blood they sank when placed in water.

Doctors scrambled to develop an effective vaccine but none was found, and they could not cure patients once they contracted the disease—all they could do was keep them hydrated, rested, and warm. Some victims fell back on folk remedies, gargling with everything from chlorinated soda to a concoction of sodium bicarbonate and boric acid. Onions were used as treatment and prevention, as was sprinkling hot coals with sulfur or brown sugar to create "curing" vapors.

Denver's first victim of the flu was Blanche Kennedy, a student at the University of Denver who died on September 27, 1918. Others soon followed. Doctors advised people to wash their hands and to refrain from spitting, to cover their mouths when coughing, and to avoid crowds. But the flu swept unchecked through Denver. The waiting lists for hospital beds spilled onto page after page, and the names of the deceased appeared daily in Denver's newspapers. Bodies were stacked like cordwood in mortuaries and buried in mass graves. Doctor William Sharpley, Denver's manager of health, ordered churches, theaters, and schools to close. A week later he banned outdoor gatherings.

The rate of fatalities in Denver spiked in late October then began to decline in early November. The plague, it seemed, had passed. On November 11, 1918, the day the treaty officially ending World War I was signed, Dr. Sharpley lifted his closing orders and his gathering ban. This didn't mean much, as no one would have paid any attention to the orders and bans anyway because of the frenzy of joy induced by Armistice Day. Jubilant Denverites packed downtown streets. Thousands filled Denver's City Auditorium to listen to speeches expressing the collective relief that the long and bloody war was finally over. Theaters reopened to entertain celebratory crowds.

These celebrations were short-lived, unfortunately, because a second wave of Spanish flu was spread by all the public gatherings in downtown Denver. As fatalities increased Dr. Sharpley again closed schools and churches in an effort to slow the soaring death rate. In addition, he ordered people to wear gauze masks when they were riding streetcars and shopping. Many people ignored these rules, however. The flu seemed so potent and deadly to Denverites that they believed any measures they took to protect themselves would be futile. The mayor of Denver, expressing skepticism over the city's ability to enforce the mask rule, stated, "Why, it would take half the population to make the other half wear masks." Crowds continued to gather in public and few people wore masks. Dr. Sharpley, realizing his rules were meaningless if the public wouldn't follow them, gave in. He allowed churches and schools to reopen and he removed the order for people to wear masks in public.

The death rate peaked during the second week of December, when more than two hundred Denverites died. But by the third week in December, the death rate began to decline dramatically—in fact, there was only one additional death during the month. The flu had run its course, and the worst health epidemic in American history was finally ending. The virus vanished as quickly as it had appeared.

Spanish flu sickened 25 percent of the U.S. population before it abated. It killed more Americans than World War I, World War II, Korea, and Vietnam combined. In Denver, more than thirteen thousand people caught the flu. And at least fifteen hundred of these perished, including the daughter-in-law and grandson of Buffalo Bill Cody. Those who survived the epidemic in Denver, such as Katherine Anne Porter, were profoundly changed because of the suffering they had endured and the carnage they had witnessed. The virus that caused the outbreak was not identified until the 1930s, long after the epidemic had ended. But the effects of the Spanish flu on Denver's ravaged population lingered well after that, often emerging in the nightmares of people who'd suffered molten fevers and uncontrollable bouts of chills, and who'd watched their loved ones die. Small wonder that Porter chose to tell her famous story of Denver's flu epidemic in a series of dreams and nightmares, and to send her main character on a terrifying journey accompanied by a grim and pale-faced stranger, who clearly represents Death.

THE RISE OF THE KU KLUX KLAN

- 1921 -

IT WAS THE SPRING OF 1921 WHEN A TALL MAN in a tailored suit stepped off a train at Denver's Union Station. William Joseph Simmons, the Imperial Wizard of the Knights of the Ku Klux Klan, had come to meet with a group of prominent Denver residents.

Six years before his trip to Denver, Simmons and fifteen of his followers had revived the Klan in Georgia. Simmons claimed that his Klan was different from the group that had harassed and lynched newly freed slaves in the post–Civil War Reconstruction South. Simmons marketed his "new Klan" as a group of patriots fighting for old-fashioned American values and crusading to maintain law and order in the chaotic wake of World War I.

The Denver residents who met with Simmons thought that what he was proposing would be just the thing to put a stop to the city's rampant vices of bootlegging, moonshining, prostitution, and gambling. Simmons's Klan would also capitalize on the fears of Denver's whites that the city's eight thousand African-Americans might rise up and demand their rights. When ten African-American students at East High School attended a graduation dance, outrage spread throughout the city. One white student was quoted by the *Denver Post* as saying, "We are not objecting to the Negroes attending the same schools with us, but to allow them to take part in our dances and formal school affairs on an equal social plane with us seems going a bit too far." The climate was right in Denver for the Klan to spread its message of bigotry.

After Simmons initiated prominent Denverites into the Klan, they formed a Denver chapter that they nicknamed the Denver Doers Club. The club announced its formation on June 17, 1921, in an advertisement in the *Denver Times*, "We are a law-and-order organization assisting, at all times, the authorities in every community in upholding law and order. . . .We are not only active now, but we were here yesterday, we are here today and we shall be here forever." The Klan began burning crosses at rallies held at South Table Mountain in the foothills of the Rockies west of Denver. The flat summit of the mountain had a good view of the city below, where the Klan planned to spew its fiery rhetoric and message of terror. Soon they were parading down Denver's streets in broad daylight in white hoods and robes.

The Denver Doers Club grew into the Kolorado Ku Klux Klan, which the *Denver Post* called "the largest and most effectively organized political force in the state of Colorado today." The founders of the Denver Doers Club canvassed the state, organizing local chapters and looking for recruits for the Klan's Invisible Empire among Protestant ministers, Masonic lodge leaders, farmers, ranchers, factory workers, and politicians. Membership grew quickly and the Denver Klan chapter soon claimed seventeen thousand members from all walks of life. People ranging from day laborers to politicians paid a ten dollar initiation fee. A white hood and robe cost an additional fifteen dollars.

Crosses were burned on Denver lawns. An African-American man was ordered to leave town. A Jewish lawyer was kidnapped and beaten. Denver Klansmen publicly smoked CYANA "Catholic You Are Not an American" cigars. The Klan exploded a bomb in the front yard of a house at 2112 Gilpin Street, shattering the windows. Walter Chapman, an African-American postal worker, had challenged Denver's racial status quo by renting this house in the middle of a white neighborhood. Unharmed by the blast but shaken, Chapman abandoned the house. Another African-American man bravely rented it. It was bombed again.

People of color were not the only targets of the KKK. Klansmen shouted obscenities from their cars as they drove through Jewish neighborhoods on West Colfax Avenue. Colorado's 125,000 Catholics, because of their large numbers, received the lion's share of Klan hatred. In an effort to harass them, the Klan tried to convince politicians to ban sacraments of wine, an important part of Catholic communion. Though the ban never took effect, the Klan's economic intimidation was effective. Their boycotts of Catholic-owned businesses and their harassment of merchants in order to convince them to fire Catholic employees caused Denver's large Catholic community financial hardship.

John Galen Locke, after receiving a medical degree from the University of Denver medical school and then being refused a license by the local medical society, took control of the Denver KKK and became its Grand Dragon. Described by a *Denver Post* reporter as "large of body and of head," Locke adorned his chubby fingers with diamond rings, draped his office door with an American flag, and filled its walls with daggers, swords, and armor. He organized groups of Klansmen to knock on the doors of supporters and tell them for whom they should vote. Locke's henchman handed out "pink tickets" that labeled each candidate as a Protestant, a Catholic, or a Jew.

Because of Locke's political engineering, Clarence Morley, an obscure Denver District Court judge and high-ranking Klan officer, became governor of Colorado. After he was elected, Morley immediately appointed two hundred Klansmen as prohibition agents giving the Klan a state-sponsored group of thugs to do its work of intimidation and harassment. A Klan member named Rice Means won a United States Senate seat. With Klan support, Ben Stapleton became mayor, and with Locke running his campaign in a later recall election, he triumphed during that test of his authority. "I will work with the Klan and for the Klan in the coming election, heart and soul," Mayor Stapleton announced at a Klan rally. "And if I am re-elected, I will give the Klan the kind of administration it wants."

Though the editor of the *Denver Express* was outspoken in his condemnation of the Klan, other newspapers such as the *Rocky Mountain News* and the *Denver Times* didn't speak out against the group. The *Denver Post* condemned the Klan—until Locke threatened the publisher, who changed his stance and ran an article praising the KKK. Not everyone in Denver supported the Klan, or kept quiet about it, however. Denver Mayor Dewey Bailey, who was in office when the Klan first announced its presence in the city, publicly criticized the hate-mongering group. Denver District Attorney Phillip Van Cise crusaded against the Klan using undercover agents to infiltrate the organization. He gathered enough evidence to send the Klan before a grand jury, but it returned a month later with no indictments.

As quickly as the Klan had seized power in Denver and throughout Colorado, they lost it, not because of public outrage or because of the efforts of law enforcement—because of turmoil within the organization. Grand Dragon Locke, who hadn't paid income taxes in more than a decade, was investigated by the United States Treasury for his management of Klan funds. And Locke, whose domineering attitude had turned many former supporters against him, made a serious misstep when he had his hooded thugs kidnap a nineteen-year-old Klansman who had allegedly gotten his girlfriend pregnant and then refused to marry her. Locke threatened the young man with castration unless he acted honorably and married her. With this cutting remark, Locke succeeded in forcing the frightened young Klansman into proposing marriage but failed miserably in fostering an image of a man devoted to dignified law and order. What little support Locke had remaining soon shriveled away. Mayor Stapleton, who had backed the Klan merely because it would help his political career, turned on Locke, convincing the national Klan headquarters to force the Denver Grand Dragon to resign. Locke's removal split the Denver Klan into fractious groups, spelling its doom as a political power in Colorado.

By the early 1930s Denver had tumbled into the depths of the Great Depression. The desperate need for jobs and the frantic search to find ways to feed starving citizens dimmed the strange and disturbing memory of the Klan's control of Denver. As if to let the city know that the KKK's brief reign of terror had not merely been a bad dream, however, hooded Denverites burned a cross on the gravesite of John Locke in Fairmount Cemetery. The fiery cross atop the former Grand Dragon's grave sent a clear message: If you were not a native-born Protestant with white skin, the Klan did not welcome you in Denver, regardless of whether the Klan was openly running the city's political machine or was hiding in the shadows behind the public spotlight.

THE DENVER MINT ROBBERY

- 1922 -

THE GUARD BURST THROUGH THE DOOR of the Denver Mint, his gun at the ready, breath puffing in the cold December air. As buckshot peppered the building, he dove for cover beneath an armored truck, wrenching his shoulder against the pavement. His pain was muted, however, by the adrenaline caused by the shotgun blasts around him and by the sight of his friend, a fellow guard named Charles, slumped on the steps of the Mint with a puddle of blood widening around him.

Often considered one of the most daring and mysterious armed robberies in American history, the Denver Mint heist was committed in broad daylight. And though the police announced that they knew who the culprits were, no one ever served a day in jail for the crime.

Denver was no stranger to bank robberies. A man had once walked into the office of the president of Denver's First National Bank, pointed a revolver at him, and brandished a bottle he said contained nitroglycerin, threatening to blow the bank to smithereens.

The extortionist made away with $20,000 in bills and $1,000 worth of gold—and he was never caught.

The Denver Mint was hit twice prior to the infamous shootout in 1922. A young clerk named Clark stole gold bars and treasury notes from the Mint's safe, then bought a horse and fled. Despite ditching a ten-pound bar that was weighing him down, Clark was captured and brought back to Denver. Most of the stolen loot was recovered, including gold that Clark had hidden in his boots. The heavy bar he'd abandoned was found by two scoundrels who sawed it in half, pounded out the mint marks, and then sold one chunk of it to a bank in Central City.

Another inside job at the Mint netted a smaller amount of money than The Denver Mint Robbery of 1922, but was no less daring. A Mint employee named Orville Harrington managed to steal away with $80,000 worth of pure gold in the form of coin manufacturing by-products known as "anodes." A secret service agent trailing Harrington caught him burying the stolen anodes in his yard. Newspaper reporters speculated that Harrington had hidden the gold in his wooden leg. Though this was never confirmed, the theft became known as "The Wooden Leg Robbery."

Despite this history of heists, Denver considered the United States Mint at 320 West Colfax Avenue the most secure building in the city. No one ever expected it to be robbed by armed thugs. (And in a way, these unsuspecting citizens were correct in their sense that the thieves wouldn't rob the building itself.)

A Federal Reserve bank truck pulled up outside the Denver Mint building on West Colfax Avenue at about 10:40 A.M. on December 18, 1922. The undersized Federal Reserve Bank nearby used the Mint's vaults to store overflow currency. On the morning of December 18, $200,000 in crisp new five-dollar bills was scheduled to be transferred from the Mint to the Federal Reserve, about twelve blocks away. It was bitterly cold and a dusting of light snow lay on the ground. As guards stepped outside the front doors of the Mint into the frigid morning and began loading the Federal Reserve armored truck with two sacks of cash, each containing $100,000, a black Buick touring car pulled up. Two men jumped out and took cover behind telephone poles. They started firing sawed-off shotguns, spraying the Denver Mint and nearby buildings. While the guards were distracted by the rain of buckshot, a third robber took advantage of the chaos and swiped the bags of money from the Federal Reserve truck and threw them into the getaway car. More guards from the Mint ran outside. They pulled their guns and started to return fire at the robbers, riddling their car with bullets. Windows shattered all around and the stone of the Mint building was pocked by bullet holes.

Federal Reserve guard Charles Linton, age sixty-five, was caught in the crossfire. Shot in the chest, he fell to the ground, already dying. The bandits sped away. Within a minute and a half of pulling up alongside the Denver Mint building in their Buick, the robbers had vanished—with $200,000 in cash stashed in their car. Guards were sure they'd shot one of the gunmen. Police, hoping the wounded man would turn up somewhere in Denver seeking medical treatment, covered the city in a massive dragnet operation. Three weeks later a dusty Buick was discovered in a garage in Denver's Capitol Hill neighborhood. Lying in the front seat was the blood-splattered and frozen body of Nick Trainor, alias J. S. Sloane, a felon who had recently been released from the Nebraska State Penitentiary on parole, and a member of the Harold Burns gang. Trainor's body was filled with bullets from the guards' guns.

Secret Service agents got to work trying to solve the case and to apprehend the other robbers. Because the Federal Reserve reissued the bills that had been taken and used the same serial numbers, tracing the stolen money was almost impossible. In addition, methods of identifying criminals were primitive by today's standards. A bloody shotgun that had been abandoned by the robbers at the Mint proved a dead end. There was no DNA analysis of a crime scene, and even fingerprinting wasn't in widespread use at the time. In the days before Social Security numbers and electronic databases, bank robbers simply changed their names, and sometimes their appearances, and then moved to new cities far away from the crimes they'd committed.

A year after the robbery, agents did manage to mount a sting attempt to nab a gang they believed had committed the crime and had then fled to Minnesota. The agents recovered $80,000 of the missing cash in the basement of a banker's house in St. Paul, but no arrests were made. It was rumored that the rest of the money had been laundered in St. Paul for half its value and was still in general circulation.

In 1925, federal agents announced that they had solved the crime, but they released no details to the public. Nothing else was mentioned until 1934 when Denver Police Chief A. T. Clark stated that a gang from the Midwest had pulled off the heist and then fled to the Minneapolis–St. Paul area. He said that the robbers had given the money to a prominent Minneapolis attorney—who was never charged. Five men and two women had pulled off the crime, the police chief claimed. Only two of the suspects were still alive and both were already serving life sentences for other crimes. No charges were filed against them. In fact, no charges related to the robbery were filed against anyone, ever.

Officials at the Denver Mint resented that the robbery was associated with their institution. Instead of "The Denver Mint Robbery," they preferred to call it "The Robbery of the Federal Reserve Bank Truck in front of the Denver Branch of the U.S. Mint." The Denver Mint Robbery, which according to eyewitnesses was "one of the most carefully planned and executed examples of ruthless banditry in the history of the West," became one of America's most famous unsolved crimes. The daring theft bred rumors, and legends grew from the mystery surrounding the case. The *Denver Post* claimed the holdup was led by Tommy O'Connor, a "notorious Chicago gunmen," along with Roy Sherrill, an escapee of Leavenworth penitentiary and a "nationally known desperado." Some said Harvey Bailey, one of the 1920s most infamous bank robbers, had masterminded the Denver Mint job. Bailey claimed that he was innocent, but the allegation followed him to his grave.

The money was never recovered and to this day it is unknown who committed the Denver Mint robbery of 1922.

CONSTRUCTING MOFFAT'S DREAM

- 1927 -

WHEN HE HEARD LOOSE ROCK SPILLING DOWN from the shaking roof, the miner ran for his life. He dodged a rolling boulder, hopped over a pile of fresh debris, and ducked under a sagging roof beam. Coughing on rock dust, he stumbled outside into the light, squinting after eight hours in a tunnel that had nearly taken his life—again. He smacked the dust from his pants and spat it from his mouth, then went to his tent to rest. He'd go back into the tunnel tomorrow, in part because he needed the good wages the job paid but also because he was proud to be building an important piece of Denver's future.

Two of Denver's rivals—Cheyenne, Wyoming, to its north, and Pueblo, Colorado, to its south—had direct rail links to the west. City leaders believed that for Denver to prosper it had to have a rail line that connected it directly to Salt Lake City and California. The problem was what lay between Denver and California: the imposing barrier of the Rocky Mountains. No one had yet attempted to conquer the Continental Divide with a train track. David Moffat, a pioneer general store owner turned bank president and mining mogul, set out to change that.

Using his vast personal fortune and the capital of investors, Moffat began the riskiest venture of his career: He started building the Moffat Road, a rail line rising over the Rockies. This was in a time of intoxicating confidence and dizzying economic expansion caused by a gold boom. Moffat and other business leaders in Denver were certain their city was destined to become a great metropolis. All they needed was a direct link to the West.

At tremendous expense, a temporary track was built over Rollins Pass at 11,660 feet—the highest railroad pass in North America. Excursion trains carried thrill-seeking tourists up the many hairpin turns and lofty trestles as it climbed toward what was being billed as "the top of the world." The train also delivered snow to the city on the Fourth of July for snowball fights (to the delight of Denver's children and adults alike). But because of the cost of snow removal from the tracks, Moffat's rail line over Rollins Pass was expensive to operate. Avalanches buried the tracks and blizzards often closed the line for days at a time. It was not unusual for travelers to be stranded on trains in the dead of winter. Some passengers prepared for the worst, bringing along snowshoes and extra food.

Moffat envisioned avoiding these problems by boring a tunnel through the Continental Divide, but he couldn't raise the funding required to build the tunnel project. He didn't live to see his railroad dream become a reality. When Moffat died in 1911 (by his own hand, it was rumored), he was bankrupt and his railroad went only as far as Craig, Colorado.

After Moffat died, however, interest in building a tunnel through the mountains continued, and in 1914 a Denver bond issue was approved to finance the construction cost. But the bond issue was defeated in courts. Not until eight years later in 1922 did the

Colorado state government pass a bill to fund a tunnel improvement district, and construction finally got under way.

From the onset of drilling, it was obvious that the tunnel was going to prove as hard to build as it had been to finance. Conditions on the west side of the mountain were much worse than anyone had imagined. Instead of the solid stone that builders had anticipated, they found crumbly rock and loose soil. As they began the slow and tedious process of boring into the mountainside, underground pressures caved in the sides of the tunnel. The ceiling sagged, the floor uplifted. Wood beams were assembled into a massive network to shore up support throughout the tunnel and keep it from collapsing.

Construction camps were set up on both sides of the Continental Divide and construction of the tunnel proceeded from both east and west. The camps were like small cities: they had dining halls open twenty-four hours a day to feed hungry workers and their families; they had houses, schools, and hospitals; they offered recreation such as boxing matches, dances, and drama clubs. Pay was good, but the work was difficult and dangerous. Workers labored in eight-hour shifts, and work went on twenty-four hours a day. A typical shift entailed drilling into rock, blasting rock, and "mucking," or removing the rock debris. Carpenters came along after the initial digging, building a support network of timbers.

Two tunnels were dug side by side: the main railroad tunnel and a small borehole running parallel to the main tunnel. The small tunnel, known as the "pioneer bore," went ahead of the main tunnel and drilled into unexplored rock, testing its solidity before work crews forged ahead with the railroad tunnel. The pioneer bore was connected to the railroad tunnel by crosscuts that sheltered men and machines during dynamite blasting. Debris from the railroad tunnel was hauled out through the pioneer bore as the work crews pushed farther into the mountain. A system of giant blowers and fans was installed at both portals to keep the air inside breathable.

Even when conditions were good, each eight-hour shift made only a few feet of progress. Unexpected events slowed things down even further. The construction crew at the west portal was plagued by unstable rock—workers often heard it spilling down and had to run for their lives. But just when engineers were about to give up and put a stop to the project, a man named George Lewis invented the Lewis Traveling Cantilever Girder, a clever contraption that supported the roof of the tunnel while workers dug out the floor and set support timbers along the sides. Using Lewis's device to lessen the danger of collapse, construction continued. But despite this new technology, in July 1926, 125 tons of rock smashed down from the tunnel's loose roof, killing six men.

Work crews at the east portal encountered solid rock, but they had other problems. In February 1926, as builders blasted near Crater Lake, underground streams began to trickle into the tunnel. As the men moved deeper into the mountain, all of Lower Crater Lake poured through a fissure, filling the tunnel with icy water. Engineers rushed in pumps to drain the flood. When they were just about finished removing the water, a snowstorm knocked out power lines supplying the pumps. The tunnel, soggy with standing water, turned to mud. The mud hardened; work crews had to excavate their way through the mess before they could continue drilling into rock and advancing the tunnel.

Undaunted by rotten rock, underground water, and sticky mud, crews continued the massive undertaking of joining the east and west portals. Though they missed the target completion date of 1926— the fiftieth anniversary of Colorado statehood—crews on both sides of the tunnel in early 1927 could hear each other's dynamite blasts. A race began to find out who could break through first. This massive tug-of-war reinvigorated the sagging spirits of the workers burnt out from all the demanding labor and difficulties they'd endured. The contest ended with the west portal crew being declared the winner as they blasted through the last wall of rock. The official "holing through" ceremony, however, had to wait a few days.

On February 18, 1927, President Calvin Coolidge set off the final blast by pressing telegraph buttons in Washington, D.C. The event was broadcast by radio across the nation, and a fascinated public listened to the final dynamite roar that pierced the backbone of the continent, completing one of the great engineering triumphs in American history and securing Denver's position as a major transportation hub.

The Moffat Tunnel finally opened for train traffic, eliminating the problems that went with the mountain railroad over the Continental Divide. Trains passed through the tunnel unbothered by the storms raging twenty-four hundred feet above them on the jagged, snowbound crest of the Rockies. And instead of climbing a 4 percent grade with many sharp turns, trains puffing out of Denver traveled a straight route with a maximum 2 percent grade. The tunnel opened northwestern Colorado's coal fields to Denver's factories and shortened the distance between Denver and the Pacific. David Moffat's vision had been fulfilled.

At the time it was finished, the Moffat Tunnel was the longest tunnel in the United States, and some engineering enthusiasts went so far as to call it one of the seven man-made wonders of the world. Nearly $18 million had been spent constructing the tunnel—$11 million more than the original estimate. At this extravagant cost, and at the human toll of twenty-eight dead laborers, a railroad tunnel twenty-four feet high, eighteen feet wide, and more than six miles long had been built. The amount of material work crews excavated—three billion pounds of rock—could have filled 1,600 freight trains, each forty cars long. The blasting had involved 2.5 million pounds of dynamite. More than 700 miles of holes had been drilled. The timber used to shore up the tunnel, if placed end to end, would have stretched 2,000 miles, covering two-thirds of the distance between New York and San Francisco.

Throughout the golden era of Colorado railroads, trains with names such as "Panoramic," "Mountaineer," "Exposition Flyer," "Prospector," "California Zephyr," and "Yampa Valley Mail" plied the Moffat Tunnel's storied tracks, transporting millions of travelers. The tunnel was important during World War II when as many as thirty trains a day passed through, hastening the movement of troops across the country as the nation readied itself for war. After World War II, as trucking and air travel eclipsed train travel as the most important forms of transportation in the country, the Moffat Tunnel—and rail travel throughout Denver and Colorado—declined in importance.

In 1979 the tunnel was declared a National Historic Civil Engineering Landmark by the American Society of Civil Engineers. Today, the site of the original Moffat Road rail line that climbed over the Rockies is a popular scenic hike. Trains loaded with coal from western Colorado continue to pass through the Moffat Tunnel and then through Denver on their way to East Coast power plants. And trains departing Denver's Union Station transport tourists westward through the long dark passageway, sending their valuable cargo to the Winter Park ski area, through the resort town of Glenwood Springs, and on to the West Coast.

WATER FOR A THIRSTY CITY

- 1936 -

GEORGE BULL WALKED THROUGH THICK GROVES OF ASPEN. Working his way up a hill, gasping in the high-altitude air, he stopped at an overlook to marvel at the expansive view of North Park spread before him. He studied something he'd just purchased for Denver, something more precious than gold. Water. The Fraser River, snaking its way through lush mountain meadows, was the key to Denver's future.

Denver had a problem. It was located on the east side of the Continental Divide along a treeless brown plain choked with dust, and most of the water the city needed lay on the other side of the Rockies.

From the town's beginnings as a gold camp until its development into a supply town for mountain mines, water from the South Platte River and Cherry Creek had met Denver's meager needs. But as smelters and factories were built and the city expanded without a sewer system, the South Platte became so polluted that it spawned a typhus epidemic. A reservoir was built southwest of Denver to store the pure waters of the Platte upstream from the city. A ditch with lateral canals down every Denver street was constructed to irrigate the grass, lilacs, and vegetable plots that replaced the cactus, sage, and gamma grass native to the high plains. Horse-drawn water wagons rolled down Denver's streets, distributing life-giving liquid to the town's citizens. But as Denver began to sprawl along the arid prairie beyond the river's banks and the reach of the canal system, it became clear that the town would soon outgrow its water supply, however carefully it was conserved, however efficiently it was used. Denver's ambitious boosters refused to see their town simply as a tiny settlement along the South Platte—they had much greater plans in store. To fulfill these plans they had to have more water.

Denver's South Platte contained 10 percent of the state's water; the Colorado River to the west of the Continental Divide carried 70 percent. Standing in the way of this aquatic bounty was the two-mile-high spine of the Rocky Mountains. Accustomed to insurmountable odds, the young city decided it would simply have to find a way to force water on the West Slope of the Rockies to flow uphill, over the Continental Divide, and down to the thirsty plains of eastern Colorado.

People in communities on the west side of the Rockies were not happy with the plans of Denver to drain their liquid resources. They claimed that this "water theft" would limit their own growth in the future.

The Denver Water Department (DWD) was formed to tap statewide water for the city, and it immediately undertook the monumental task of redirecting water from one side of the Rockies to the other. The DWD dispatched engineer George Bull to western Colorado to prospect for water. He secured the rights to flows in the Blue River near Dillon and the Fraser River in North Park. Denver now owned all the water it needed. But how to get it from west of the Rockies to east of the mountains? Reversing gravity was too difficult even for brash, industrious Denver.

The answer to this logistical problem lay hidden two miles beneath the stony crests of the Rockies. The Moffat Tunnel, a more than six-mile-long engineering marvel, allowed trains to pass under the imposing mountains rather than over them. The work crews that built the Moffat Tunnel had drilled a "pioneer bore," a small tunnel that workers used to forge ahead of the railroad tunnel so they could probe the geology of the mountain and clear away debris from blasting. This pioneer bore had been of no use to Denver after trains began traveling through the main tunnel. The long, skinny bore had fallen into disrepair as its sides caved in and its ceiling sagged. The DWD proposed cleaning the rock rubble out, reinforcing its walls and roof, and lining it with concrete so it could transport water to Denver.

The idea was well received. The drought that had created the Dust Bowl nearly emptied Denver's reservoirs, motivating the city to begin readying the pioneer bore to bring water to the desperate city. One thousand men worked for more than a year improving the bore. When the project was complete, Denver had, in a sense, succeeded in drawing water from rock. As flow from the Fraser River passed through the tunnel in 1936, radio stations broadcast the sound of water, and people across the country listened to the gurgle that would put an end to Denver's Dust Bowl days. "DREAM OF AMPLE WATER IS REALITY AT LAST" proclaimed the *Denver Post*.

Though the pioneer bore had been neglected for many years, Denver had originally intended for it to divert water—the Moffat Tunnel was never meant to be solely a railroad project. Railroad engineers had recommended the city build a shorter and cheaper tunnel higher up in the mountains at 9,930 feet above sea level, 2.6 miles long, and at a cost of $4 million. But the city ignored this advice and built the tunnel more than 800 feet lower, at 9,100 feet, 6.2 miles long—and at a staggering cost of $18 million. The reason for this decision, many disgruntled West Slopers claimed, was that the lower, longer and costlier tunnel would be able to capture more of the runoff from western Colorado's water supply and send it east to the sun-parched plains of Denver.

"Pioneer bore" proved an apt name: The small tunnel had originally cleared the way for Denver to become one of the nation's major railroad hubs. Now the tunnel allowed the city—thirsty for water and hungry for growth—to tap the vast liquid resources it needed to expand. Following the lead of the pioneer bore, dozens of other projects soon passed beneath the Continental Divide to draw West Slope water into Denver, including the Big Thompson project to the north of the city, and the Roberts Tunnel to the south. A vast system of tunnels, pipelines, siphons, and reservoirs made possible Denver's extraordinary growth as it swelled into a major urban center in the second half of the twentieth century.

The pioneer bore continues to provide much of the city's water, moving more than 800 million gallons toward Denver each day. And the potential for future growth of the Denver metropolitan area into the twenty-first century still resides in the rivers of western Colorado and water that nature had destined to flow toward the Pacific side of the Continental Divide.

WINE BARRELS SAVE WINTER PARK

- 1938 -

A CROWD OF SKIERS BUNDLED IN PARKAS, their eyes goggled against the bright light of a Colorado bluebird winter day, gathered around a tow lift. As the motor sputtered to life, its sound was muffled by the blanket of snow that lay across Winter Park. The powder was dry and knee deep—prime skiing conditions. The skiers couldn't wait to get to the top of the hill. When the lift was set in motion for a test run, it moved without a problem—until skiers sat down on the seats, immediately stalling the lift. Engineers decided there simply wasn't enough power to haul the weight of skiers uphill. But there was fresh powder just waiting to be skied. Something had to be done.

From the time of the gold and silver rushes, Denverites had been traveling into the mountains to glide along on hand-hewn skis with tips steamed into upward curls. A single long pole was used by prospectors to balance and brake as they glided through the mountains in search of precious metal. Mail carriers used skis to traverse from town to town when they made their rounds in the hills outside of Denver.

In the early 1900s Colorado skiers started sliding downhill at Steamboat Springs and Hot Sulphur Springs. Winter carnivals featuring ski racing became popular throughout the state. Carl Howelsen, known as "The Flying Norsemen" and famous for his circus act of leaping on skis waxed with soap over the backs of elephants, popularized the sport of ski jumping in Colorado and introduced skiers to the concept of ski bindings that attached their boards to their boots—putting a stop to runaway skis careening toward people on the slopes below. A tow lift pulled skiers to the top of a slope at Crested Butte, and a rope tow was built near the summit of Berthoud Pass. Denverites filled cars by the thousands and drove up dizzying Berthoud Pass to seek thrills in the abundant snow alongside the road.

When Denver started work on Winter Park in 1938, the sport of skiing really took off. The *Rocky Mountain News* collaborated with the Denver Chamber of Commerce and ski enthusiasts to form the Colorado Winter Sports Council. Local skiers wanted more access to mountain slopes; city boosters thought Denver was missing out on a great opportunity to tap tourist dollars by developing European-style ski resorts. The Colorado Winter Sports Council convinced the city to lease from the United States Forest Service thousands of acres of mountainous terrain near the West Portal of the Moffat Tunnel, a train passageway that went beneath the rocky spine of the Continental Divide. The city later purchased this land and named it Winter Park. Some of the world's best skiers, including Dartmouth's esteemed ski coach Otto Schneibs, visited Winter Park and raved about the quality of its slopes.

Denver's Manager of Improvements and Parks proposed developing the Winter Park area at the West Portal of the Moffat Tunnel into a "winter playground that would be the world's best." City leaders agreed, envisioning it as the centerpiece of their Mountain Parks

System, an ambitious undertaking that aimed to preserve vast tracks of land to the west of Denver where its citizens could play in the mountains. Local business owners donated money for the development of lifts, ski runs, and shelters; city workers volunteered their weekends to clear the slopes. A Public Works Administration grant from the federal government added more funds, and labor from the Colorado Mountain Club, the Civilian Conservation Corps, and the United States Forest Service made possible the creation of Winter Park.

Trails were freed of brush and debris, and construction proceeded smoothly. But then a glitch arose with the primitive tow lift on its inaugural run. A resourceful Denverite offered a clever solution. After deciding that the thick metal plates on the seats of the lift were adding too much weight, he went home to Denver and collected wine kegs from his cellar. He hauled the kegs back to Winter Park, asking the workers to remove the heavy steel plates on the lift chairs and replace them with lightweight wooden keg staves. (Some enterprising Colorado pioneers had fashioned keg staves into skis, but wood staves had never been used as part of a ski lift.) Test runs proved successful; the lightened lift moved dozens of people at a time to the top of the slope. The ski area soon opened to the public, and after paying one dollar for lift tickets, skiers were hauled uphill. When they reached the top and slid off the "wine barrel lift chairs," they had their choice of three runs to schuss down.

The Denver and Salt Lake Railroad soon began running "snow trains" from Denver through the Moffat Tunnel to its West Portal, where skiers were dropped off at the slopes of Winter Park. The train ride and the skiing were both enormously popular with Denver's residents, and the sport soon caught on with tourists. While Winter Park remained the centerpiece of Denver's Mountain Parks System, other ski areas soon opened throughout the state. As highway and air travel replaced trains and made the ski areas easily accessible, skiing replaced summer recreation as the showpiece of Denver's booming tourist-based economy.

Today, Winter Park is the third-largest ski area in Colorado, boasting over 2,886 skiable acres, two terrain parks, a half pipe, and "Discovery Park," where novices can get familiar with the slopes. The wine barrels that saved Winter Park gave birth to an industry that earns Denver billions of dollars a year. The gold seekers who once scoured the mountains in search of precious metal have been replaced by pleasure seekers. The light and plentiful Colorado powder craved by skiers and snowboarders the world over has proved through the years more valuable than mining. And the rich lode of Rocky Mountain snow—unless climate change alters the weather—will keep producing "white gold" year after year.

THE CREATION OF RED ROCKS

- 1941 -

DENVER'S MAYOR STAPLETON WALKED A PATH through Red Rocks Park, admiring the way the red sandstone formations contrasted against the clear blue sky. Breathing deeply, he inhaled the scent of pine pitch. He told George Cranmer, the man who was walking with him, that this was a perfect rock garden and it should be preserved in its natural state forever. Cranmer, Denver's Manager of Improvements and Parks, looked at the sandstone towers and looming walls of Red Rocks and decided he would blow them up.

Three hundred million years ago, turmoil deep below the earth's surface thrust up great ledges from the bed of a prehistoric ocean. Erosion by wind, frost, and rain sculpted the uplifted stone. Exposed layers bright with pink, rust, and crimson pigments would come to hint at the shores of ancient seas and debris left over from ancestral mountains. Dinosaur tracks from the Jurassic would tell of a period 160 million years before when the terrible creatures had prowled what are now the streets of suburban Denver. The fossils and formations found at Red Rocks stretch the imagination. Bones of flying reptiles and giant sea serpents poke from the ground. Ship Rock, the size and shape of a huge ship, lies balanced on another boulder so delicately the enormous slab of stone sways in the wind.

Before Europeans stumbled upon Red Rocks, the Utes used the area for spiritual ceremonies. The tall walls of stone formed a perfect natural shelter, and the elevated location gave the Native Americans who gathered there a commanding view of the plains below. They held their ceremonial dances on a natural stage of flat rock, and their singing and the beat of their drums echoed from the gigantic stone formations surrounding them.

The United States Army Expedition of Stephen H. Long brought the first whites to record the impressive pieces of red sandstone in 1820. A professor who several decades later searched the area for skeletons during Colorado's "Great Dinosaur Bone Rush" described the rocks as "many remarkable and weird shapes full of cavernous holes and crannies." Red Rocks, which for a time was considered one of the Natural Wonders of the World, delighted those Denverites who made the trek outside of town to see the formations. The area was called at first "Garden of the Angels," and later "Garden of the Titans," and distinctive features were given names such as "Angels' Bathtub," "Demons' Grotto," "Roasted Goose," and "Sleeping Lion." In addition to gazing at the rocks, Denver's citizens absorbed a breathtaking two-hundred-mile-wide panoramic view of their city and the surrounding plains.

John Brisben Walker, founder of *Cosmopolitan* magazine, bought the land where the Red Rocks amphitheatre would eventually be built and opened it to the public. Masses of people from the city flocked there by horse, train, and car. Walker dreamed of musicians one day performing on a stage tucked into the enormous rock outcroppings. He organized concerts on a temporary platform.

Three decades later, George Cranmer watched a performance at an amphitheatre in Taormina, Sicily, that had been built by ancient Greeks. Recalling the impressive acoustics he'd heard as a boy at John Walker's Garden of the Angels, Cranmer wondered if something similar to the Greek amphitheatre could be built at Red Rocks Park—which the city of Denver had renamed after purchasing the land from Walker for the paltry sum of fifty-thousand dollars.

Cranmer, denied funds by the city to do the project (and aware that Mayor Stapleton would not be pleased if the rock garden he loved was tampered with), came up with a clever scheme. He tapped the labor pool of the Civilian Conservation Corps (CCC), a relief program created by President Franklin D. Roosevelt to put unemployed young men to work constructing buildings, trails, and roads. Cranmer used his political connections in state and local government to get three hundred men from a CCC group to build his amphitheatre at no cost to the city of Denver. Next, Cranmer obtained materials from the National Park Service. To help build roads and parking areas near the amphitheatre, he secured more laborers from the Works Progress Administration, a "make work" program similar to the CCC.

With all the labor and materials he needed, Cranmer faced his next hurdle: how to complete the project without upsetting the mayor. For several days while the mayor was out of town, Cranmer had CCC laborers put dynamite charges under boulders. Then, when the explosives were in place, all at once the many tons of rock rubble that were cluttering the area were blown up. What remained when the dust of the pulverized boulders cleared was an open space between two magnificent sandstone outcroppings, Creation Rock to the north and Ship Rock to the south.

A section of the mayor's rock garden had disappeared, but in its place Denver architect Burnham Hoyt designed a seating arrangement for ten thousand people that would be in harmony with the natural surroundings. Narrow slabs of sandstone were used to make the seats for concertgoers. Concrete and steel were concealed underground to stabilize the stage and strengthen the orchestra pit. Cranmer assumed the three-hundred-foot-high monoliths of stone would make perfect sounding boards. The theatre, with its natural red outcroppings of stone offset by native green junipers, was undeniably beautiful, but when the outdoor theater opened for its first concert in 1941, the acoustics weren't quite right.

Cranmer flew on his own dime to Germany where he tried to convince Wolfgang Wagner, son of the famous composer Richard Wagner, to visit Denver with him. Wolfgang agreed. He toured Red Rocks and suggested changes, and he refused the money Cranmer offered to pay him for his advice, calling Red Rocks so "worthy a cause." Based on Wagner's advice, improvements such as wind walls were added to the stage, creating "perfect acoustics."

John Walker's vision was fulfilled. City parks manager George Cranmer and architect Burnham Hoyt had used their creativity and ingenuity to combine Colorado's natural beauty with the acoustical properties of an open-air auditorium. The result was a concert venue unlike any other in the world. New York's Museum of Modern Art and the American Institute of Architecture called Red Rocks "Colorado's finest twentieth century building." Mayor Stapleton was at first distraught that his beautiful rock garden had been dynamited and turned to a music stage, but he learned to appreciate the amphitheatre as it became a world-famous music venue and garnered widespread attention for the city.

Music performances at Red Rocks have thrilled Denverites for decades. Lucky concertgoers have absorbed the sounds of classical and jazz, country and rock. Red Rocks has hosted musicians ranging from jazz legend Nat King Cole to country icon Willie Nelson, from opera star Lily Pons to notorious rocker Ozzy Osbourne. The Beatles, the

Mormon Tabernacle Choir, The Grateful Dead—the list of world-class performers who have appeared at Red Rocks is long, and the venue's unique stage has served as the setting for music video classics such as U2's "Under a Blood Red Sky."

Following World War II, Red Rocks began hosting, in addition to concerts, local church services such as baptisms, christenings, and ordinations. Especially popular were sunrise services on Easter Sunday. Denver had rediscovered the beauty, both acoustical and spiritual, that Native Americans had enjoyed centuries earlier when they danced and beat their drums amid the three-hundred-million-year-old rocks.

JAZZ AND
"A CERTAIN RACY WILD SMACK"

- 1947 -

IN SEARCH OF INSPIRATION, JACK KEROUAC HITCHHIKED to Denver, arriving on Larimer Street in the summer of 1947 with "the most wicked grin of joy in the world." That Denver summer would change American culture profoundly and forever.

The term "Beat Generation" was used by Jack Kerouac to mean a generation of young Americans who were worn out and world weary, but also upbeat and "on the beat," similar to musicians keeping time to the rhythm of a wild and beautiful song. In a three-week burst fueled by coffee and Benzedrine, Kerouac wrote *On the Road,* regarded today as the definitive story of the Beat Generation. Though it took him a mere three weeks to put it on paper, Kerouac had been laying the groundwork for the story for years. Much of his preparation time was spent in Denver, where in the summer of 1947 he hung out with a man named Neal Cassady.

Raised in a busted-knuckle, blue-collar neighborhood in Denver, Neal Cassady was a talented car thief and a charming con artist who spent much of his earlier years in reform schools and juvenile detention centers. When Cassady wasn't stirring up trouble with his friends in Denver, he could be found in libraries throughout the city reading books and studying philosophy. He could hotwire a car and quote from the writings of Kant—and sometimes he did both at the same time.

In the Denver Public Library, Neal Cassady met a native Denverite named Hal Chase. Chase told Cassady about a New York group of Beat artists and writers he'd met as a student at Columbia. Cassady was intrigued by Chase's stories about these rebels who had no use for the everyday American world of suits, ties, and quiet suburban homes. Stealing a car and speeding it down Denver's streets was something of a quest for enlightenment, almost a religious search, for Cassady, who also rejected the "falseness" of the nine-to-five daily grind in favor of a more "authentic" life based on following his impulses, wherever they led.

When Hal Chase returned to college at Columbia, he told Jack Kerouac all about Cassady's ideas and antics. Kerouac was fascinated by this book-reading, philosophizing Denver car thief. He read letters Cassady had penned while in reform school, and was impressed with their ideas and energetic style. Kerouac became determined to meet the man who'd written them. After Cassady road-tripped to New York, the two men became fast friends. When Cassady left New York and went back to Denver, Kerouac, thinking Cassady might be the main character for a story already brewing in his head, followed the wild young man west.

Kerouac quickly became part of Cassady's crew of Denver misfits, gamblers, and pool players who took joyrides in stolen cars, smoked dope on the grounds of Elitch Gardens, and hung out with homeless people on the State Capitol lawn. The group soon included not only Kerouac but also Allen Ginsberg, a poet who, along with Kerouac, popularized the Beat movement in America. While in Denver, Ginsberg helped found the "Jack Kerouac School of Disembodied Poetics at Naropa," located in nearby Boulder.

Kerouac and Ginsberg felt at home in Denver. The nightlife of Larimer and Curtis Streets offered plenty of pool halls with cheap eats and abundant beer, Benzedrine, and marijuana. Also, there was a thriving music scene in the African-American neighborhood of Five Points, filled with clubs that hosted jazz greats such as Billie Holliday and Duke Ellington. While in Denver Kerouac was on the lookout for material. His observations and experiences, recorded in tiny dime-store notebooks, became the basis for *On the Road*, which immortalized Cassady as Dean Moriarty, a magnetic conman who burned with energy. The book was based largely on Kerouac's thoughts and escapades while prowling Denver with Cassady. "In the men's room, Dean and I punched the door and tried to break it but it was an inch thick. . . . In the foyer outside the saloon old former prospectors sat dreaming over their canes under the tocking old clock." In one of the most famous passages of *On the Road*, the narrator stands on Denver's Welton Street "feeling that the best the white world had offered was not enough ecstasy for me, not enough life, joy, kicks, darkness, music, not enough night."

Kerouac also befriended a Denverite named Ed White, who became another character in Kerouac's books. But more importantly, White was credited by Kerouac as being the first person to suggest he start "sketching" with words. Kerouac took White's advice and began writing down what he saw and felt quickly and without critical thought. This process felt right to him, and he continued to create stories in this impulsive way, trying to capture the true essence of experience and not dilute it with too much intellectual brainwork.

Soon Kerouac had developed his own jazzy, improvisational style; this unique way of writing set *On the Road* apart from other books being published at the time. Kerouac had done something most serious writers aspire to do: He'd created something truly new, both in terms of content, with the criminal-philosopher character based on Denver's Cassady, and in terms of style, influenced by Denver's Ed White.

In the summer of 1947, Allen Ginsberg also found himself quite taken with the vibrant, charismatic Cassady, who talked fast, lived in the moment, and penned stream-of-consciousness letters with thoughts that sprawled across dozens of pages. While staying at Denver's Colburn Hotel a few blocks south of the Capitol, Ginsberg became lovers with Cassady, and he wrote a cycle of poems called "Denver Doldrums." Cassady and Ginsberg frequented Charlie Brown's Bar in the basement of the Colburn, and in their hotel room at night they used Benzedrine to stay awake till the sun rose, talking about philosophy and their lives. Ginsberg tapped his experiences at the Colburn to create poems such as "The Green Automobile" and "Howl." In "The Green Automobile" Ginsberg writes, "Denver! Denver! we'll return / roaring across the City & County Building lawn. . . ."

The Beat Generation, often considered the first modern subculture in the United States, spread across the country and had a tremendous impact on American life. The original seeds of the movement sown by Kerouac and Ginsberg influenced all forms of alternative American culture that have sprung up since the Beat first began in Denver in the summer of 1947. As the decades passed, "beatnicks" turned into "hippies," and then morphed into "punks."

And the movement can be traced backward as well as forward— some say the Beat movement really began with Walt Whitman, a rebellious American poet who used an energized, almost frantic style of writing and had no qualms about breaking the rules of literature or society in his relentless quest for enlightenment. Whitman, too, was influenced by the time he had spent in Denver, a young, rowdy frontier town he praised in *Speciman Days,* published in 1882, as having "a certain racy wild smack, all its own."

Denver today is home to a slew of poets and writers, and the "Jack Kerouac School of Disembodied Poetics at Naropa" draws students from around the country. Much like a repeating jazz riff, Denver's beat, both in American literature and in American popular culture, goes on and on.

SAVING MOLLY BROWN

- 1970 -

As a thunderous roar filled the saloon, the man reached for a whiskey glass that had begun to slide across the bar top. He blinked his eyes and stared out a window. Hadn't there been a building across the street a few minutes before? Now there was a cloud of dust, nothing more. The man shook his head, then emptied his glass and told the bartender to refill it. Might as well have one last drink, he thought. The bar he was sitting in was scheduled to be demolished the next day.

The Molly Brown House stands at 1340 Pennsylvania Street, a reminder of an era in Denver when Victorian splendor reigned supreme. In 1886 the Large family, after amassing a substantial fortune in silver mining, commissioned an architect to build a fabulous dream home in Denver's swanky Capitol Hill neighborhood. The architect combined various styles, including Classic Queen Anne and Richardsonian Romanesque, into an eclectic masterwork. The rugged rhyolite rock of the façade contrasted with smooth sandstone, and the lavish interior was adorned with stained glass windows, elaborate woodwork, and exquisitely painted ceilings. Just after the house was finished, the Larges lost their fortune in the Silver Panic and the Browns moved in.

Margaret Tobin Brown, from modest origins in the river bottoms of Missouri, was a trailblazer who worked passionately for women's suffrage and social justice. Newly rich from her husband's bonanza in gold mining, she set sail in 1912 on the most fashionable of boats, the *Titanic*. When the *Titanic* sank, Brown heroically saved other passengers from drowning and gained world-wide fame when she was immortalized as *The Unsinkable Molly Brown* on stage and screen. Fifty-eight years later, Historic Denver, Inc. heroically saved her house.

In Denver in the 1960s, Victorian homes were not popular. In fact, any "old" structure standing in the city had a good chance of being battered with a wrecking ball or bulldozed to make room for high-rise apartments and parking lots. "Urban renewal" was the name of the game, and the Denver Urban Renewal Authority demolished block after city block, systematically leveling much of downtown Denver's city core. There seemed no end to the number of buildings that would tumble. When native Denverites ventured toward their "renewed" downtown, many became disoriented because so many familiar landmarks had disappeared.

One Denver resident finally had enough. Afraid there wouldn't be a single historic piece of architecture left standing, Helen Arndt decided to do something. She got herself appointed to the Denver Planning Board (the first woman ever to do so) and joined with other concerned citizens to create a local landmark commission modeled after those in East Coast cities such as Boston and New York. Denver's mayor was leery of this idea, and some politicians felt it might hamper progress, but according to Arndt, "a remarkable lot of Denver citizens of all ages, from ninety to about ten, stood up and said they didn't like to see their city torn apart."

City leaders granted Arndt's request, creating the Denver Landmark Preservation Commission, a group with the power to recommend landmark designation for buildings of historical, architectural, or geographical merit. If the City Council approved a building as a landmark, it could be spared the wrecking ball and bulldozer. Thanks to Arndt's vision and persistence, in its first thirty years the commission she had helped create saved over three hundred individual landmarks throughout the city, as well as thirty historic districts.

Similar to Arndt, Dana Crawford became distraught when wrecking balls began smashing everything in sight, and also like Arndt, Crawford decided to do something about it. One day while shopping for antiques downtown she realized that many of the second-hand stores and pawnshops where she was browsing were antiques themselves—she believed the buildings were beautiful and worth saving to share with future generations. Crawford spearheaded an effort to restore Larimer Square, steeped in the lore of Denver's early days. In 1970, in an effort to save Molly Brown's house from the wrecking ball, she joined with Arndt to help found Historic Denver, Inc.

After Brown died her house was turned into a home for wayward girls. Later it was converted to a boarding house for single men. By 1970 the house was slated for demolition to make way for a modern office building. Historic Denver, Inc. made numerous appeals in the media for funds, and they gained the support of thousands of Denverites, including the mayor's wife. They raised enough money to purchase the house and restore it. Historic Denver, Inc.—fifteen hundred members and two hundred volunteers strong a year after forming—used microscopic paint analysis, architectural research, and the study of original house photographs to convert the run-down Brown house into an attractive museum. It's a memorial to the boomtown economy of Denver, recalling the young town's optimism and "rush to respectability." Details of the Molly Brown house's décor, from stone statues of lions crouching outside the front door to a polar bear rug lying on the parlor floor, have been preserved. Many of the Browns' possessions have been donated to the museum and are on display; visitors can gaze at items ranging from Victorian undergarments to a Tiffany tea set.

Saving the Molly Brown house in 1970 was a watershed moment in Denver's historic preservation movement, marking the start of a widespread understanding that some monuments to the past had more value than the skyscrapers or parking lots that would replace them. Historic Denver, Inc. built on its initial efforts and piled up an impressive list of preservation successes, including saving and renovating the Paramount Theatre, one of the last survivors of downtown Denver's grand art deco movie palaces. They also relocated the house of Dr. Justina Ford, an African-American pioneer physician who broke through the double barrier of gender and race to become lovingly known as Denver's "Lady Doctor." After the Ford house was moved away from a demolition zone where developers planned to put a parking lot, it was restored and then turned into the Black American West Museum and Heritage Center located at the southwest corner of Thirty-first and California Streets.

Today, Historic Denver, Inc. has grown into one of the largest private preservation groups in the country. The Molly Brown House Museum draws forty thousand visitors a year, each one of them learning something about historic preservation and the unsinkable dreams of the people in Denver who would not stand to see all the old buildings of their city fall.

THE BLAST HEARD ROUND THE CITY

- 1973 -

THE DENVER POLICE DEPARTMENT OFFICER DUCKED behind a Volks-wagen Beetle just as a bullet whizzed past his shoulder. He slid two fresh rounds in his pistol, took a deep breath, and stepped out from behind the Beetle, crouching low to run through the smoke and haze of gunpowder. He threw a glance at the windows above him. Where was the sniper hiding?

Some believe Denver's Crusade for Justice was a dangerous organization responsible for a rash of bombings during the 1970s. Others see it as a positive influence that allowed Hispanic political activists to air their legitimate grievances. One thing is certain: After a building at 1547 Downing Street exploded shortly after midnight on March 17, 1973, Denver was never the same.

Rodolfo "Corky" Gonzales, a former bar owner, bail bondsman, and well-known professional boxer from the barrio, wrote a poem called "I Am Joaquin" in which he blended his identity with those of his heroes, Pancho Villa and Emiliano Zapata. Both the poem and

Gonzales's desire to advocate for the civil rights of people of Mexican descent resonated with Denver's Mexican-American community. After working as a Democratic political leader and the director of an anti-poverty program, Gonzales became disillusioned and abandoned mainstream politics in order to advocate on his own for people of Mexican descent. Appealing to their cultural nationalism, he called for the creation of Chicano-controlled communities separate from the rest of Denver. During a speech at a demonstration outside City Hall in 1966, Gonzales said, "We are on a crusade for justice." The title stuck, and a movement was born.

The Crusade for Justice (*La Crusada Para la Justicia*) aimed to create a Chicano society based on humanism instead of what Gonzales saw as Anglo materialism. It called for the reform of the police and courts, improved housing and employment opportunities for people of Mexican ancestry, and education specifically tailored to the needs of Chicanos. The crusade set up headquarters in a large and imposing building, the former Calvary Baptist Church on Sixteenth Avenue and Downing Street. From there Gonzales edited a newspaper, *El Gallo*. Dissatisfied with the public school system, Gonzales and his followers started their own school, the Escuela Tlatelolco. Staffed by volunteers, it gave free bilingual classes and lessons in Chicano culture to children. It also offered a vast array of community facilities including a nursery, a gym, a Mayan ballroom, legal aid offices, and a "Revolutionary Theater."

As Gonzales's ideas were spreading through college campuses and barrios around the nation, an event that occurred in the spring of 1973 made the movement impossible for the city of Denver to ignore.

On March 17, along the 1500 block of Downing Street in front of Crusade headquarters, Denver police officers used a rarely enforced city ordinance to arrest a man for jaywalking. An angry crowd gathered to protest the arrest, and a fierce gunbattle soon erupted. Staccato pops sounded in the night as supporters of the Crusade and police traded bullets. A *Denver Post* reporter who was caught up in the firefight described it this way: "There wasn't time for thinking or even for the luxury of being afraid. All you did was run for cover."

Just after midnight, Officer Steven Snyder of the Denver Police Department and Luis Martinez fired back and forth at each other in an alley near Sixteenth and Downing. After being shot in his side and leg, Officer Snyder killed Martinez with a shot to the head. Snyder's partner then radioed for help. As soon as other officers arrived on the scene, they were fired upon from snipers in the windows of nearby apartments. Wounded, the officers retreated just moments before the second story of the Downing Terrace apartments, owned by the Crusade, exploded.

An enormous blast tore a gaping hole in the upper floors of the building and lit up the night skyline. The lungs of onlookers were filled with acrid smoke. Bricks and rubble rained down, pelting officers who'd ducked for cover beside a pair of Volkswagen Beetles. A war veteran who witnessed the carnage commented on how disturbing it was to experience the sights and sounds of combat in his own city.

When the debris from the building settled and the fighting finally ended, one man was dead and nineteen people, including twelve police officers, were injured. Thirty-six people were arrested. Police accused the Crusade of storing explosives in the apartment building. "It was a regular arsenal inside," said one detective after noting the weapons and dummy hand grenades investigators recovered from the rubble. Gonzales claimed his organization's participation in an American Indian Movement march had prompted the FBI to manipulate the Denver police into forcing the confrontation at Crusade headquarters; he also charged that police grenade launchers had caused the explosion. Gonzales proclaimed Martinez, the man shot dead by the police officer, a Chicano hero and a martyr for their cause. Crusade members saw themselves as victims of the bomb blast. The media, and most Denverites, disagreed.

The explosion next to Crusade headquarters began a quick unraveling of the organization's influence. Denver's citizens started viewing members of the Crusade as anarchists, not political activists. This growing perception was reinforced when police arrested two men in a plot to blow up a police substation in southwest Denver; one of the men arrested was a Crusade member who was caught transporting a bomb. Crusade thugs, frustrated with all the negative publicity surrounding their organization, began beating up Chicanos who didn't back the movement. These violent rampages convinced many moderate people of Mexican descent that the Crusade for Justice was a radical and dangerous group that didn't deserve their support. The Crusade soon collapsed.

Despite the disturbing history of violence associated with the movement, it did help bring concern for the rights of people of Mexican descent to the attention of Denver. The Crusade provided several important services to the Chicano community, including combating drug abuse and educating dropouts. The school it founded still educates students in grades 7–12 and is run by Nita Gonzales, Corky's daughter. Today, thanks in part to the Crusade for Justice, political activism among Denver's Hispanic community is alive and well. Hispanics have served in Denver as police chief, fire chief, and manager of safety—and in 1983, Federico Peña was elected as the city's first Hispanic Mayor.

THE EVENT THAT DIDN'T HAPPEN

- 1976 -

AFTER MEETING WITH THE INTERNATIONAL OLYMPIC COMMITTEE in Amsterdam, a group of triumphant Denverites were hailed as heroes when they returned to Colorado. Denver had been awarded the coveted prize of hosting the Winter Olympics of 1976, the centennial year of Colorado's statehood. Coloradans had been working toward this goal for decades, and finally it was going to happen—the Olympics would put Denver on the world map. The group that had made this possible was greeted downtown by a brass band and a motorcade. Celebrating citizens crowded the streets, and the air was filled with honking horns and happy shouting.

Soon, however, Denverites became alarmed at the potential costs of the Games—both in dollars and in environmental damage.

From the start there was confusion about where events would be held, and many people grumbled that city boosters, when trying to entice members of the International Olympic Committee, had overstated Denver's proximity to the mountains. The United States Forest Service proposed Copper Mountain as the best Olympic site—despite the fact that it was far from Denver and there were no ski towns nearby to house people. Some said the most logical plan was to use the slopes of Winter Park and run special trains to transport athletes and spectators from Denver to the ski area. Others argued for events to be held across a huge swath of area far larger than any previous Winter Olympic venue: from Denver to Steamboat Springs, the Games would span more than 160 miles.

When Evergreen was named as the location for cross-country events, residents of the relatively low-elevation town in the foothills of the Rockies pointed out that the mild climate and unpredictable snowfall of the area might lead to poor skiing conditions. Concerns about epic traffic jams and noxious pollution as spectators shuttled between events gave Denverites pause, and many citizens voiced their fears that more people would be lured into moving to the pristine mountains and plains of Colorado. A *Denver Post* columnist summed up this point of view, "The trouble with tourists is that, having looked around, many wish to return . . . and we already have sufficient people lousing Colorado up."

The International Olympic Committee made its position clear to Denver from the start: If Coloradoans refused to help finance the cost of the Games, they would be moved to Innsbruck, Austria.

The issue was put to Colorado voters. The language on the ballot was considered by many to be confusing—"No meant yes and yes meant no," explained one member of the Denver Organizing Committee, which was in charge of promoting the Olympics in Denver. Committee members also admitted to being complacent: They were so elated by the prospect of having the Games in their city that they didn't realize that losing the ballot measure was a possibility, and they failed to make their case strongly to Denver's voters.

Anti-Olympic groups made a strong case for their own cause, citing reports of financial losses from cities that had hosted previous

Games. With a rebellious young lawyer named Dick Lamm raising questions about Denver hosting the Olympics, many workers began to see what the Winter Games would do for the city and certain businesses, but not how it would benefit them individually. They saw real estate developers getting rich by building new ski resorts and erecting "cardboard cities" to house visitors; they saw themselves paying their hard-earned tax dollars to finance the Olympics and then having to deal with the environmental effects of millions of people trampling their beloved mountains and open spaces.

With estimated costs of the Games soaring, on November 7, 1972, Denver voters rebelled at the ballot box against the plans of the Denver Organizing Committee. A solid majority—more than 59 percent—said they weren't willing to spend tax dollars to have Denver host the Games. The Winter Games were moved to Austria. No city, state, or nation had ever before turned down the Olympics. And it hasn't happened since.

The Olympic controversy boosted Dick Lamm's career; the landmark vote put him in the media spotlight, which helped him win the governorship of Colorado two years later. While Lamm was in the governor's mansion and the Games were being held in Austria, new ski resorts were developed all over Colorado's mountains. And the anti-Olympics vote certainly didn't put a halt to environmental problems in the Denver area. The city's population surged as newcomers from Southern California and other coastal areas were drawn to Colorado for the clean air, abundant open space, and prime recreational opportunities. Denver soon emerged as one of the healthiest and fastest-growing cities in America. As Denver's reputation as a mecca for the health-conscious and outdoor-oriented grew, the influx of people led to the conversion of wildlands to parking lots and shopping malls, and pollution plagued the city. Denver soon earned the dubious distinction of having one of the highest per-capita licensed motor vehicle ownership rates in the world. The city had more auto registrations than adult residents, and a brown cloud caused primarily by auto exhaust hung in choking billows across its skies.

Many Denverites who had voted to reject the 1976 Winter Olympic Games—because of fears they'd lead to excessive growth and environmental problems—ask themselves today if they did the right thing. Some, including Dick Lamm, maintain that voting to reject the Olympics was the right thing to do regardless of the fact that every environmental problem foreseen due to the Games has come to pass—even without the Olympics coming to town.

Colorado bid on the 2002 Winter Games but lost out to Salt Lake City, Denver's main rival in the contest to lure winter sports enthusiasts to mountain resorts. Some say Denver's hopes of hosting the Games were dashed forever by the non-event of 1976.

THE GREAT AIRPORT GAMBLE

- 1989 -

On a warm September day in 1989, Mayor Peña thrust his shovel into a wheat field, symbolically putting Denver at the center of the nation's transportation map. Officials at the groundbreaking ceremony spoke of "the world's greatest airport" and "the planet's largest inland port."

The mayor, city boosters, and business officials all claimed that the new airport would be the solution to the financial woes of a city still reeling from an oil bust. Denver's population had been declining relative to other cities in the West, particularly Dallas. Denver had a bad case of airport envy: Dallas had a big airport; Denver wanted a bigger airport.

But before the city could build Denver International Airport, it would have to close down Stapleton International, which would make Denver the first city in United States history to shut down a major, fully functioning airport. Critics—both from outside the city and within it—said the scheme was ridiculous.

This was neither the first time Denver had gambled on its future nor the first time it had taken a chance on building an airport. Mayor Stapleton, when he took office in 1923, believed air travel was the way of the future. He didn't want to see Denver surpassed by other cities with airports. Not everyone in Denver shared Stapleton's belief that air travel would eclipse train travel, however. Many saw flight as simply a hobby of the rich, not a potential mode of transportation for the masses. The *Denver Post* called the mayor's purchase of barren land ten miles from Denver's central business district "Stapleton's Folly" and "Simpleton's Sand Dunes." But Stapleton stuck to his guns and saw his plan through and, in 1929, an airport with two dirt runways opened for business. The people who mocked the mayor for his air-travel dream had no idea that within sixty years Stapleton International Airport would become, for a brief time in the mid-1980s, the fifth-busiest air passenger hub in the world.

But this wasn't enough for a restless Denver, trying to find ways to prop up its economy. While Denver was watching Dallas enjoy prosperity due in large part to its large airport, Salt Lake City snubbed Denver by taking out full-page ads in the *New York Times* and other prominent newspapers. The ads showed a flustered business executive arriving late for a meeting and apologizing by saying, "Sorry I'm late but I had to fly through Denver."

Denver responded to this smear from the City of the Saints by getting to work on plans for the most extravagant airport the nation had ever known—an airport so large, so modern, so impressive, Denver would become an air travel giant and the envy of Salt Lake City and Dallas and every other city in the Western United States. The world's biggest airport would show the oil-rich Texans and those cheeky upstarts in the Beehive State what Denver was made of.

Though air-passenger traffic was declining at Stapleton in the late 1980s, boosters of a new airport spread a convincing message throughout the city: If Denver built a giant airport similar to the Dallas–Fort Worth airport (but even bigger), the project would promote the economic growth the city so desperately needed and would secure Denver's place as a major transportation center. The new airport seemed a wild dream; but just as Mayor Stapleton's dream had paid off by allowing Denver's ski industry to boom by making room for people to fly into the Rockies, the new airport would make Denver a "world class city" and an air travel hub for the twenty-first century.

Not everyone was convinced. Critics said that the airport was too far from Denver's city center "in the middle of nowhere." They complained that Denver had failed to work out the details of a rail transit system covering the vast distance between the airport and its downtown and the commute by car would increase traffic and pollution on the highways. Others complained that the project was unnecessary and scrapping a perfectly good airport was absurd. Nevertheless, Denver International Airport was approved by voters in Adams County, allowing Denver to annex the land where the airport was to be built—an area twice the size of Manhattan.

The plans called for a fifty-three-square mile airport, the largest in the world—larger than Chicago's O'Hare and Dallas–Fort Worth combined. It was, simply, the largest piece of real estate dedicated to commercial aviation on earth. It would be located far from the city core to reduce noise impacts and to allow for massive expansion in the future. Runways would be built extra long to compensate for Denver's thin high-altitude air. (The Mile High City's rarefied atmosphere provides less lift for airplane wings than sea-level air— so planes in Denver need more runway length for takeoff than they do in Dallas.) Four enormous concourses would be connected by "the most efficient ground transportation system at any airport in the world." The terminal was to be perched atop a man-made mesa constructed by displacing one-third the amount of earth moved to dig the Panama Canal. The terminal's roof was to be made from Teflon-coated fiberglass fabric erected into giant tent-like cones that would glow at night and be visible from one hundred miles away, recalling Colorado's snowcapped Rockies as well as the teepees Native Americans had pitched upon the plains.

But problems slowed progress to a crawl. Airlines threatened to sue to put a stop to the construction, claiming the new facility would increase their landing costs and force them to raise prices. Critics attacked Denver's financial claims, arguing that airport construction would go way over the amount the city had estimated. The Federal Aviation Administration (FAA) came to Denver's defense, announcing that the new airport was needed to end flight delays and dangerous congestion in the nation's airspace. The FAA endorsed the project and promised hundreds of millions of dollars in federal aid. After the Feds came to the rescue, construction continued.

In late 1989, Mayor Peña finished his final term as governor and handed over control of the city that had undertaken—either boldly or foolishly, depending on whom you asked—one of the largest public works projects in recent history. Mayor Wellington Webb inherited the airport-in-progress. Denver International Airport (DIA) was scheduled to open in October of 1993, but changing demands by United Airlines forced Mayor Webb to extend the opening date, first to December 1993, then to March 1994. A mill wright strike at the airport slowed construction further, and the opening day was pushed out again—this time to the middle of May 1994.

In April of 1994, just before the scheduled grand opening, Denver received the national attention it craved—but not for the reasons it had hoped it would. Reporters the city had invited to watch the first test of what had been hailed as the most sophisticated high-tech computerized baggage system on the planet rolled their cameras and scribbled furiously in their notepads as clothing, toothbrushes, and shoes were strewn beneath the automated tracks of the system. Bags and suitcases were ripped open and flung right off the rails. This was not a promising start for what Denver had billed as "the world's greatest airport," and the press was not kind in its comments about the bungling baggage system. Mayor Webb canceled the grand opening date of mid-May.

After many embarrassing delays, on a snowy day at the end of February 1995, sixteen months behind schedule and at a cost of $5.3 billion (initial cost projections had been $1.5 billion), DIA finally opened its runways. Despite colossal cost overruns, a dysfunctional baggage system, complaints from art critics about the misuse of DIA's massive public art fund to purchase bad art, allegations of political corruption, kickbacks and cronyism—even investigations by the FBI and SEC—a corps of volunteers wearing white cowboy hats greeted passengers as they stepped from planes. The passengers navigated new terminals and concourses so shiny and futuristic with their whooshing subway cars and tent-like roofs pouring light into the vast spaces of the skyport, DIA did indeed seem an airport of the future and a magnificent monument to Denver's ingenuity and vision. DIA was dubbed "the largest, most technologically advanced airport on earth," and it soon became the fifth-busiest airport in the United States and the tenth-busiest airport in the world. The jets roaring through Denver's skies ensured the city's future as an important travel hub, much as trains puffing across its plains once had when the young town built its first railroad.

IF YOU BUILD IT, THEY WILL COME

- 1993 -

THE COLORADO ROCKIES OPENED IN THE Denver Broncos' Mile High Stadium on April 9, 1993 before 80,277 fans—the most to witness an opening game in Major League Baseball history. The vast majority of those fans had driven downtown from the suburbs. Many of them, however, would soon move to the city. Baseball and bold city planners were about to change Denver forever.

After World War II, thousands of Denverites fled the urban landscape in pursuit of the American dream, and Denver's suburbs were born. Ranches and farmland disappeared as shopping malls and subdivisions filled up the open prairie. While new development sprawled across the plains, Denver's inner core emptied and quickly deteriorated. The once-bustling lower downtown district became synonymous with urban decay. Its rampant poverty and crime reinforced suburbanites' dislike of the area—lower downtown Denver became something to avoid. Shopping centers were built in the suburbs for the convenience of residents, new freeways were constructed to service the burgeoning communities, and businesses relocated away from the city center so that commuters could travel shorter distances to work. Denver's lower downtown district turned to a ghost town. Its brick buildings stood abandoned along empty streets while traffic clogged the freeways in outlying areas.

Lower downtown became as empty as when it had been founded more than a hundred years earlier. In the early days of Denver, many structures of sturdy brick had been built. A century later the Denver City Council found these buildings worthy of preservation. Originally designed as business headquarters and to house the goods and supplies passing through Denver by rail, buildings along Wynkoop, Market, and Wazee Streets were characterized by granite foundations and walls of many-colored brickwork. The elaborate cornices, Romanesque arches, art deco designs, cast metalwork, and terra-cotta accents that graced the warehouses and offices were emblematic of the city's pride and ambition. Inside the buildings, some of which had served as corporate headquarters during Denver's boom days, were enormous rounded cement columns, ornate woodwork of pine and oak, pressed metal ceilings, and beautifully tiled floors. Covered loading docks and old rail spurs hinted at Denver's history as a great industrial and supply center for the West.

The Lower Downtown Historic District was formed in March 1988, saving the area from "urban renewal," a project responsible for leveling many of the city's old buildings in the 1960s and 1970s. A zoning ordinance that included height limitations on buildings and strict design guidelines for rehabilitation and new construction protected the historic character of the district. So the area was preserved, but it was still empty—until baseball came to town.

After Denver was awarded a Major League Baseball franchise, the Colorado Rockies, the team broke a dozen attendance records—including the most single-season fans (4,483,350) to attend any

American sport. This enthusiasm prompted planners to increase inaugural Opening Day capacity at Coors Stadium by more than six thousand seats. Instead of locating the stadium in the outlying suburban areas of Denver where most of the population lived, city planners boldly chose to build it in the heart of Denver's empty lower downtown, banking on the belief that "If you build it, they will come."

The grass-field stadium, located two blocks from Denver's historic Union Station at Twentieth and Blake Streets, was made of hand-laid brick and was topped with an old-fashioned clock tower above its main entrance. Coors Field combines the amenities of a modern stadium with the atmosphere of an old-time ballpark, complementing the aura of Denver's rich past in the lower downtown. Fans sitting near first base and in the right-field area are treated to a view of the Rocky Mountains—something no other Major League stadium can boast.

The Rockies, during their first year in the new ballpark, made the National League playoffs and Coors Field quickly established itself as the most prolific ballpark for sluggers. In 1999, The Rockies and their opponents combined for 303 home runs, the most ever hit in a single season at one venue. The average 1999 score was a sky-high 8-7. Balls were consistently smacked into the stands as players racked up homerun after homerun, due in large part to simple physics; a baseball travels 9 percent farther in the thin air at 5,280 feet than it does in the thicker air at sea level. A home run hit 400 feet at Yankee Stadium, which sits at sea level, might travel 440 feet if hit in the Mile-High City.

The home run sluggers who filled the Rockies lineup came to be known as the "Blake Street Bombers," and as their big bats hammered balls into stands crammed full of cheering spectators, sports bars sprang up around the stadium. People flocked to lower downtown to watch the Rockies play; fans lingered after games looking for more fun. As restaurants and shops moved into the area's historic buildings, an upscale entertainment district was born. Lower Downtown, or LoDo as it affectionately became known, was soon home to more than three-hundred restaurants, ninety sports bars and brewpubs, a collection of museums, and a variety of galleries and stores. Even LoDo's Union Station, an ornate building that had been one of the busiest rail hubs in the nation, enjoyed a renaissance. It became the centerpiece of a busy regional transit system: an integrated hub for trains, buses, light rails, shuttles, taxis, bicycles, and pedestrians.

Real estate developers caught on and started converting abandoned warehouses into lofts so that hipsters enjoying themselves in bustling LoDo could avoid their commute from the suburbs. Entrepreneurs followed the lead of the LoDo loft-dwellers who'd given up the sleepy suburbs in favor of the lively lower downtown and began relocating their businesses in the area.

The success of this rejuvenated district spilled beyond the boundaries of LoDo, creating renewal in numerous blighted areas and growth throughout the city. Word spread about Denver's downtown, which combined the amenities of urban fun with outdoor adventure. You could take a train trip from Union Station into the Rockies to ski powder or bomb down a trail on a mountain bike, then catch a train back to LoDo to watch a ballgame, or eat in a five-star restaurant, or take in a show at the second-largest performing arts center in the nation. Tourists came—and many of them stayed, deciding they wanted to live where the city meets the mountains. The place where Denver had begun, after years of vacancy and neglect, had become the trendiest place in town, and Denver had gained a reputation as one of the most exciting cities in the United States.

Today, LoDo is at the heart of a vibrant urban scene and is one of the most popular—and expensive—places in Denver to live. Though the days of the Blake Street Bombers have passed, there are still plenty of homeruns hit at Coors Field to excite fans. And there are now dozens of businesses throughout LoDo that have nothing to do with baseball. For example, The Tattered Cover Book Store, after enjoying success in Denver's Cherry Creek district, opened a second store in an historic LoDo building. The Tattered Cover has grown into a nationally recognized bookseller praised by the *New York Times* as "the best general book store in the United States." And LoDo has also given rise to some major cultural centers. The Museum of Contemporary Art / Denver was opened in a renovated fish market in LoDo's Sakura Square to provide the city with, according to the museum's website, "an innovative forum that inspires and challenges all audiences and creates understanding and dialog about art of our time."

From books to baseball, from a ski train to modern art, LoDo serves up a rich buffet of entertainment and cultural options. The busy district in the birthplace of Denver now anchors a revitalized downtown, and it stands as a shining example of urban renewal for cities throughout the nation.

DENVER FACTS & TRIVIA

In 1893 Denver became the first large city in the world to give women the right to vote.

Denver is nicknamed "The Mile-High City" because of its official elevation, one statute mile (5,280 feet) above sea level. This elevation is marked on the fifteenth step on the west side of the State Capitol Building. Also, a row of seats in the upper deck of Coors Field, home of the Colorado Rockies, is marked in purple to indicate that the row is exactly one mile above sea level.

The mountain panorama visible from Denver is 120 miles long. Two hundred peaks of the Rocky Mountains, including thirty-two peaks taller than 13,000 feet, can be seen from downtown Denver.

Denver has over three hundred sunny days a year—more than San Diego or Miami Beach.

Denver averages 15.4 inches of precipitation per year, about the same as Los Angeles.

Denver's average annual snowfall is about fifty-five inches, a little more than Boston and much less than Buffalo, New York.

Denver's average February high temperature is forty-five degrees Fahrenheit, warmer than New York City, Boston, and Chicago.

The cheeseburger was "invented" in Denver by Louis Ballast, who operated a drive-in restaurant called "The Humpty Dumpty Barrel." Ballast applied for a patent on his invention in 1935.

A trip to the summit of Pikes Peak near Denver in 1893 provided Katharine Lee Bates with the inspiration to pen the lines of her famous poem "America the Beautiful."

Private charity organizations in early Denver merged into one organization, the Community Chest, which evolved into the nation's first United Way.

Denver's Emily Griffith Opportunity School, founded in 1916, is the oldest adult vocational/technical school in the United States.

Judge Ben Lindsey started the nation's first juvenile court system in Denver.

In 1886 the Denver Tramway Company gave the city America's first—and the world's second—electric streetcar system.

A Colorado railroad hired hunters, including William Frederick Cody, to feed its workers. Cody kept count of the buffalo he shot: 4,280, earning him the name "Buffalo Bill." He is buried atop Lookout Mountain, west of Denver.

In 1983 Denver elected its first Hispanic mayor, Federico Peña.

In 1991 Denver elected its first African-American mayor, Wellington Webb.

The Black American West Museum & Heritage Center in Denver estimates that nearly a third of the cowboys in the building of the American West were black.

The United States Denver Mint stamps about forty million coins a day—as many as eight hundred a minute. This adds up to eight billion coins a year that are punched, bagged, and shipped from Denver.

The United States Denver Mint is the country's second-largest gold bullion depository. It has a stockpile of solid gold bars worth $100 billion, surpassed only by what is held in Fort Knox.

Colfax Avenue, twenty-six miles long, is the longest continuous street in the United States.

The Eisenhower Tunnel in the mountains west of Denver is the highest vehicular tunnel in the world (11,158 feet above sea level).

Denver, with 205 parks, has the nation's largest city park system. Outside the city, Denver's Mountain Parks Department maintains an additional 20,000 acres, its own buffalo herd, and Red Rocks Amphitheatre.

The road up 14,260 foot high Mount Evans, maintained and operated by Denver City Parks Department, is the highest paved road in North America.

Denver is the only city in North America to have its own ski resort.

Denver hosts the world's largest rodeo each year at the National Western Stock Show.

The Denver Performing Arts Complex is the second-largest performing arts complex in the country, after Lincoln Center in New York City.

The dome of the State Capitol Building in Denver is covered with 200 ounces of 24K gold.

Denver has more than doubled in population since 1960. Its population is projected to double again in the next forty years.

The population of the Denver-Aurora metro area was recently estimated at 2,830,000, making it the twenty-third largest metropolitan area in the United States.

Denver has the tenth-largest downtown in America.

Denver has the greatest percentage of college graduates of any major metropolitan area in the nation.

Denver has the highest percentage of Baby Boomers of any major city in the United States.

Of all major American cities, Denver has the second-highest concentration of scientists and researchers.

Because Denver has the most veterinarians per capita and the fewest fleas of any metro area in America, the Purina Pet Institute rated it as the healthiest city for pets.

Denver Public Library has been named "Best Big-City Library" by Hennen's Public Library Ranking System. In per capita circulation, Denver is second only to Boston.

With the exception of Washington, D.C., Denver has more federal workers than any other metropolitan area in the nation, which has earned it the nickname "Little Washington."

Denver is one of the world's largest broadcasting and telecommunication centers. It is the only major city in the United States where single-relay, one-bounce satellite transmissions are possible to six out of seven continents in a single business day.

A federal study identified Denver as having the thinnest residents of any major United States city.

Denver likes its beer. It brews more than eighty different types, more than any other city. Coors Brewing Company in Golden, Colorado, just west of Denver, is home to the largest single-site brewery in the world. Denver has the nation's largest brewpub, Wyncoop Brewing Company. Denver claims to have the highest number of home brewers of any city and is host to the Great American Beer Festival—dubbed "The Super Bowl of Beer."

The Denver-Boulder metro area was ranked by *Forbes* magazine two years in a row as "America's Best City for Singles."

Denver hosts 8.8 million visitors each year.

In 2005 Denver became the first major United States city to legalize the private use of marijuana.

BIBLIOGRAPHY

General Resources

Abbott, Carl, Stephen J. Leonard, and David McComb. *Colorado: A History of the Centennial State.* Niwot: University Press of Colorado, 1994.

Arps, Louisa Ward. *Denver in Slices.* Denver: Sage Books, 1959.

Bancroft, Caroline. *Colorful Colorado.* Boulder, CO: Johnson Pub. Co., 1966.

———. *Denver's Lively Past: From a Wild and Woolly Camp to Queen City of the Plains.* Boulder, CO: Johnson Pub. Co., 1971.

Brenneman, Bill. *Miracle on Cherry Creek; An Informal History of the Birth and Re-Birth of a Neighborhood.* Denver: World Press, Inc., 1973.

Coel, Margaret. *Chief Left Hand: Southern Arapaho.* Norman: University of Oklahoma Press, 1981.

Colorado Writers' Program of the Work Projects Administration. *Denver, Queen of Mountain and Plain; Revised for the Use of Pupils In the Denver Junior High Schools from A Short History of Denver. Denver:* Denver Public Schools, 1945.

Conner, Daniel Ellis, ed. *A Confederate in the Colorado Gold Fields.* Norman: University of Oklahoma Press, 1970.

Dallas, Sandra. *Yesterday's Denver.* Miami, FL: E. A. Seemann Pub., 1974.

Dorset, Phyllis Flanders. *The New Eldorado: The Story of Colorado's Gold and Silver Rushes.* New York: Macmillan, 1970.

Dorsett, Lyle W., and Michael McCarthy. *The Queen City: A History of Denver.* Boulder, CO: Pruett Publishing Company, 1986.

Eitemiller, David. *The Denver Mint: From the Gold Rush to Today.* Phoenix, AZ: American Traveler Press, 2002.

Etter, Don D. *Auraria: Where Denver Began.* Boulder: Colorado Associated University Press, 1972.

Fay, Abbott. *Ski Tracks in the Rockies: A Century of Colorado Skiing.* Louisville, CO: Cordillera Press, 1984.

Fetler, John. *The Pikes Peak People; The Story of America's Most Popular Mountain.* Caldwell, ID: Caxton Printers, 1966.

Fowler, Gene. *Timber Line; A Story of Bonfils and Tammen.* Garden City, NY: Garden City Pub. Co., 1947.

Goodstein, Phil. *The Seamy Side of Denver: Tall Tales of the Mile High City.* Denver: New Social Publications, 1993.

Leonard, Stephen J. *Trials and Triumphs: A Colorado Portrait of the Great Depression, With FSA Photographs.* Niwot: University Press of Colorado, 1993.

Leonard, Stephen J., and Thomas J. Noel. *Denver: Mining Camp to Metropolis.* Niwot: University Press of Colorado, 1990.

Metcalf, Fay D., Thomas J. Noel, and Duane A. Smith. *Colorado: Heritage of the Highest State.* Boulder, CO: Pruett Pub. Co., 1984.

Mumey, Nolie. *Clark, Gruber & Company, 1860–1865, A Pioneer Denver Mint; History of Their Operation and Coinage.* Denver: Artcraft Press, 1950.

Noel, Thomas J. *The City and the Saloon: Denver, 1858–1916.* Lincoln: University of Nebraska Press, 1982.

———. *Denver Landmarks & Historic Districts: A Pictorial Guide.* Niwot: University Press of Colorado, 1996.

———. *Denver's Larimer Street: Main Street, Skid Row, and Urban Renaissance.* Denver: Historic Denver, Inc., 1981.

———. *Mile High City: An Illustrated History of Denver.* Encinitas, CA: Heritage Media Corp., 1997.

Noel, Thomas J., and John Fielder. *Colorado 1870–2000, Revisited: The History Behind the Images.* Englewood, CO: Westcliffe Pub., 2001.

Noel, Thomas J., and Barbara S. Norgren. *Denver, The City Beautiful and its Architects.* Denver: Historic Denver, Inc., 1987.

Noel, Thomas J.; photographer, Richard Whitacre. *Denver, Rocky Mountain Gold.* Tulsa, OK: Continental Heritage Press, Inc., 1980.

Perkin, Robert L. *The First Years; An Informal History of Denver and the Rocky Mountain News, 1859–1959.* Garden City, NY: Doubleday, 1959.

Quillen, Ed. Edited by Mary Jean Porter. *Deep In the Heart of the Rockies: Selected Columns from the Denver Post 1985–1998.* Westcliffe, CO: Music Mountain Press, 1998.

Ronzio, Richard A. *Silver Images of Colorado.* Denver: Sundance Pub., 1986.

Sprague, Marshall. *Colorado: A Bicentennial History.* New York: Norton, 1976.

Smiley, Jerome C. *History of Denver; With Outlines of the Earlier History of the Rocky Mountain Country.* Evansville, IN: Unigraphic Inc., 1971.

Trenholm, Virginia Cole. *The Arapahoes, Our People.* Norman: University of Oklahoma Press, 1970.

Ubbelohde, Carl, ed. *A Colorado Reader.* Boulder, CO: Pruett Press, 1962.

Ubbelohde, Carl, Maxine Benson, and Duane A. Smith. *A Colorado History.* Boulder, CO: Pruett Pub. Co., 2001.

West, Elliott. *The Contested Plains: Indians, Goldseekers, & the Rush to Colorado.* Lawrence: University Press of Kansas, 1998.

Westermeier, Clifford P. *Colorado's First Portrait; Scenes by Early Artists.* Albuquerque: University of New Mexico Press, 1970.

The Pikes Peak Gold Rush—1859

Brown, Robert L. *The Great Pikes Peak Gold Rush.* Caldwell, ID: Caxton Printers, 1985.

Rogers, James Grafton. *The Rush to the Rockies; Background of Colorado History.* Denver: State Historical Society of Colorado, 1957.

Voynick, Stephen M. *Colorado Gold: From the Pike's Peak Rush to the Present.* Cartography and illustrations by Trudi Peek. Missoula, MT: Mountain Press Pub. Co., 1992.

The Rise of Judge Lynch—1859

Leonard, Stephen J. *Lynching in Colorado 1859–1919.* Boulder: University Press of Colorado, 2002.

Gilpin's Gamble to Save the Union—1862

Alberts, Don E. *The Battle of Glorieta: Union Victory in the West.* College Station: Texas A & M University Press, 1998.

Scott, Robert. *Glory, Glory, Glorieta: The Gettysburg of the West.* Boulder, CO: Johnson Books, 1992.

The Great Fire—1863

Kreck, Dick. *Denver in Flames: Forging a New Mile High City.* Golden, CO: Fulcrum Publishing, 2000.

The Sand Creek Massacre—1864

Greene, Jerome A., and Douglas D. Scott. *Finding Sand Creek: History, Archaeology and the 1864 Massacre Site.* Norman: University of Oklahoma Press, 2004.

Hoig, Stan. *The Sand Creek Massacre.* Norman: University of Oklahoma Press, 1961.

Scott, Bob. *Blood at Sand Creek: The Massacre Revisited.* Caldwell, ID: Caxton Printers, 1994.

A Race to Build a Railroad—1870

Forrest, Kenton, and Charles Albi. *Denver's Railroads: The Story of Union Station and the Railroads of Denver.* Golden: Colorado Railroad Museum, 1986.

Noel, Thomas J. "All Hail The Denver Pacific: Denver's First Railroad," *The Colorado Magazine,* Spring 1973, 91–116.

The Hop Street Riot—1880

Dirlik, Arif, ed.; with the assistance of Malcolm Yeung. *Chinese on the American Frontier.* Lanham, MD: Rowman & Littlefield, 2001.

Ourada, Patricia. "The Chinese in Colorado," *The Colorado Magazine,* October 1952, 273–84.

Building a House of Mirrors—1889

MacKell, Jan. *Brothels, Bordellos, & Bad Girls: Prostitution in Colorado, 1860–1930.* Albuquerque: University of New Mexico Press, 2004.

Secrest, Clark. *Hell's Belles: Denver's Brides of the Multitudes: With Attention to Various Gamblers, Scoundrels, and Mountebanks and a Biography of Sam Howe, Frontier Lawman.* Aurora, CO: Hindsight Historical Publications, 1996.

The Epidemic—1918

Crosby, Alfred W. *America's Forgotten Pandemic: The Influenza of 1918.* New York: Cambridge University Press, 2003.

Iezzoni, Lynette. *Influenza 1918: The Worst Epidemic in American History.* New York: TV Books, 1999.

Porter, Katherine Anne. *Pale Horse, Pale Rider; Three Short Novels.* New York: Modern Library, 1949.

The Rise of the Ku Klux Klan—1921

Goldberg, Robert Alan. *Hooded Empire: The Ku Klux Klan in Colorado.* Urbana: University of Illinois Press, 1981.

Constructing Moffat's Dream—1927

Albi, Charles, and Kenton Forrest. *The Moffat Tunnel: A Brief History.* Golden: Colorado Railroad Museum, 2002.

Griswold, P. R. *David Moffat's Denver, Northwestern and Pacific: "The Moffat Road".* Denver: Rocky Mountain Railroad Club, 1995.

Monroe, Gregory. *Moffat!: Rio Grande-Southern Pacific-Union Pacific West of Denver, Colorado.* Arvada, CO: Fox Publications, 1997.

Water for a Thirsty City—1936

Eha, Walter R.; [prepared for] Board of Water Commissioners. *The Moffat Water Tunnel Project: An Achievement in Denver's Metropolitan Development Program.* Denver: The Board of Water Commissioners, 1936.

Eha, Walter R. *Greater Denver's Greater Water System.* Denver: Board of Water Commissioners, 1936.

Grigg, Neil S. *Colorado's Water: Science & Management, History & Politics.* Fort Collins, CO: Aquamedia Pub., 2003.

The Creation of Red Rocks—1941

Noel, Thomas J. *Sacred Stones: Colorado's Red Rocks Park & Amphitheatre.* Edited by Erik Dyce. Denver: Division of Theatres & Arenas, 2004.

Jazz and "A Certain Racy Wild Smack"—1947

Cassady, Carolyn. *Off the Road: My Years with Cassady, Kerouac, and Ginsberg.* New York: Morrow, 1990.

Cassady, Neal. *The First Third & Other Writings.* San Francisco, CA: City Lights, 1981.

———. *Collected Letters, 1944–1967.* New York: Penguin, 2004.

Ginsberg, Allen. *As Ever: The Collected Correspondence of Allen Ginsberg & Neal Cassady.* Berkeley, CA: Creative Arts Book Co., 1977.

Kerouac, Jack. *On the Road.* New York: Viking Press, 1957.

Plummer, William. *Holy Goof: A Biography of Neal Cassady.* New York: Thunder's Mouth Press, 2004.

Turner, Steve. *Angelheaded Hipster: A Life of Jack Kerouac.* New York: Viking, 1996.

Watson, Steven. *The Birth of the Beat Generation: Visionaries, Rebels, and Hipsters, 1944-1960.* New York: Pantheon Books, 1995.

Saving Molly Brown—1970

Bancroft, Caroline. *The Unsinkable Mrs. Brown.* Boulder, CO: Johnson Pub. Co., 1970.

Iversen, Kristen. *Molly Brown: Unraveling the Myth.* Boulder, CO: Johnson Books, 1999.

Walker, Elizabeth Owen. *Cast in Stone: The Molly Brown House Revealed.* Denver: Historic Denver, Inc., 2001.

Whitacre, Christine. *Molly Brown: Denver's Unsinkable Lady.* Denver: Historic Denver, Inc., 1984.

The Blast Heard Round the City—1973

Meier, Matt S., and Feliciano Rivera. *The Chicanos: A History of Mexican Americans.* New York: Hill and Wang, 1972.

Vigil, Ernesto B. *The Crusade for Justice: Chicano Militancy and the Government's War on Dissent.* Madison: University of Wisconsin Press, 1999.

The Great Airport Gamble—1989

Dempsey, Paul Stephen, Andrew R. Goetz, and Joseph S. Szyliowicz. *Denver International Airport: Lessons Learned.* New York: McGraw Hill, 1997.

Miller, Jeff; photography by Pat Olson. *Stapleton International Airport: "The First Fifty Years."* Boulder, CO: Pruett Pub. Co., 1983.

If You Build It, They Will Come—1993

Gibson, Barbara; photography by Cynthia S. Herrick. *The Lower Downtown Historic District.* Denver: Historic Denver, Inc. in cooperation with The Denver Museum of Natural History, 1995.

INDEX

Ford, Justina, 99
Fort Lyon, 31, 32
Fort Union, 17
Fraser River, 78, 80

G
Gettysburg of the West, The, 18
Gilpin, William, 15–17, 18–19
Ginsberg, Allen, 93, 94
Glorieta Pass, 18
go-backers, 4
gold rush, 1–5, 10–13
Golden, CO, 37, 38, 39, 40
goldfields, 16, 17, 18
Gonzales, Rodolfo, 100–103
Gordon, James, 7
Great American Beer
    Festival, 122
Great American Desert, 2, 4
Great Bamboozle, 4–5
Great Blizzard of 1913, 53–56
Great Depression, 66
Great Fire, 20–24
Great Pikes Peak Gold
    Rush, 1–5
growth, 106–7, 113
Gruber, Emanuel, 11

H
Harrington, Orville, 68

Historic Denver, Inc., 97,
    98–99
historic preservation, 97–99, 114
Holladay, Ben, 46
Holladay Street, 46
homicides, 7, 8
Hop Street, 41, 42, 43–44
House of Mirrors, The,
    47–48
housing, 20–21, 97
Howelsen, Carl, 83

I
immigrants, 41–44, 51
Indian Row, 45
influenza epidemic, 57–61

J
Jack Kerouac School of
    Disembodied Poetics at
    Naropa, 93, 95
Judge Lynch, 7–9
juvenile courts, 119

K
Kansas Pacific Railroad, 37–38
Kansas Territory, 3
Kennedy, Blanche, 59
Kerouac, Jack, 91, 92–94
Klein, Oscar, 53

ABOUT THE AUTHOR

Stephen Grace has worked jobs ranging from deckhand on Mississippi riverboats to neuropsychological research assistant to whitewater rafting guide. He has led numerous trips, including snowboarding adventures for at-risk youth and a volunteer project in China for college students. A resident of Colorado, he divides his free time between Denver's museums and its mountains. His first novel, *Under Cottonwoods* (The Lyons Press, 2004), was a Book Sense 76 selection. He is currently at work on a new novel.